Treating Children
and Adolescents
in Residential and
Inpatient Settings

Developmental Clinical Psychology and Psychiatry Series

Series Editor: Alan E. Kazdin, Yale University

Recent volumes in this series . . .

Treating Children and Adolescents in Residential and Inpatient Settings

Robert D. Lyman
Nancy R. Campbell

Volume 36
Developmental Clinical Psychology and Psychiatry

 SAGE Publications
International Educational and Professional Publisher
Thousand Oaks   London   New Delhi

To Kathy and Meghan   —RDL
To my parents, T. C. Campbell and
    Nora Conner Campbell   —NRC

Copyright © 1996 by Sage Publications, Inc.

For information address:

SAGE Publications, Inc.
2455 Teller Road
Thousand Oaks, California 91320
E-mail: order@sagepub.com

SAGE Publications Ltd.
6 Bonhill Street
London EC2A 4PU
United Kingdom

SAGE Publications India Pvt. Ltd.
M-32 Market
Greater Kailash I
New Delhi 110 048 India

Printed in the United States of America

Library of Congress Cataloging-in-Publication Data

Lyman, Robert D.
    Treating children and adolescents in residential and inpatient
settings / authors, Robert D. Lyman, Nancy R. Campbell.
       p.   cm.—(Developmental clinical psychology and psychiatry;
v. 36)
    Includes bibliographical references and index.
    ISBN 0-8039-7046-3 (cloth).—ISBN 0-8039-7047-1 (pbk.)
    1. Child psychotherapy—Residential treatment. 2. Adolescent
psychotherapy—Residential treatment. I. Campbell, Nancy R.
II. Title. III. Series.
RJ504.5.L95   1996
362.2'083—dc20   96-10054

This book is printed on acid-free paper.

96 97 98 99 00 01 10 9 8 7 6 5 4 3 2 1

Sage Production Editor: Michèle Lingre
Sage Typesetter: Andrea D. Swanson

CONTENTS

SERIES EDITOR'S INTRODUCTION

Interest in child development and adjustment is by no means new. Yet only recently has the study of children benefited from advances in both clinical and scientific research. Advances in the social and biological sciences, the emergence of disciplines and subdisciplines that focus exclusively on childhood and adolescence, and greater appreciation of the impact of such influences as the family, peers, and school have helped accelerate research on developmental psychopathology. Apart from interest in the study of child development and adjustment for its own sake, the need to address clinical problems of adulthood naturally draws one to investigate precursors in childhood and adolescence.

Within a relatively brief period, the study of psychopathology among children and adolescents has proliferated considerably. Several different professional journals, annual book series, and handbooks devoted entirely to the study of children and adolescents and their adjustment document the proliferation of work in the field. Nevertheless, there is a paucity of resource material that presents information in an authoritative, systematic, and disseminable fashion. There is a need within the field to convey the latest developments and to represent different disciplines, approaches, and conceptual views to the topics of childhood and adolescent adjustment and maladjustment.

The Sage Series on **Developmental Clinical Psychology and Psychiatry** is designed to serve uniquely several needs of the field. The series encompasses individual monographs prepared by experts in the fields of clinical child psychology, child psychiatry, child development, and related disciplines. The primary focus is on developmental psychopathology, which refers broadly here to the diagnosis, assessment, treatment, and prevention of problems that arise in the period from infancy through adolescence. A working assumption of the series is that understanding, identifying, and treating problems of youth must draw on multiple disciplines and diverse views within a given discipline. The task for individual contributors is to present the latest theory and research on various topics including specific types of dysfunction, diagnostic and treatment approaches, and special problem areas that affect adjustment. Core topics within clinical work are addressed by the series. Authors are asked to bridge potential theory, research, and clinical practice, and to outline the current status and future directions. The goals of the series and the tasks presented to individual contributors are demanding. We have been extremely fortunate in recruiting leaders in the fields who have been able to translate their recognized scholarship and expertise into highly readable works on contemporary topics.

In the present book, Drs. Robert Lyman and Nancy Campbell examine hospitalization and residential treatments for children and adolescents. The authors place residential treatment into a broader perspective of the overall care of youths. Different options and settings of residential care are elaborated. The principles and practical issues underlying decision making for placement of youth in such settings are also covered. Diverse models of treatment, intervention goals, and clinical services are described and evaluated. Strategies of patient care, specific interventions used within the hospital, and the integration of services during and after hospitalization are covered. The effectiveness of various treatment programs are carefully evaluated as well. Hospitalization of youth raises several issues in light of the removal of youth from the home and peers, the cost of such treatments, and the nature and effects of the services that are provided within the hospital. All of these issues are covered to convey the rationale, research, and considerations that enter into hospitalization. A very special feature is an appendix that serves as a detailed resource to learn more about inpatient programs, legal issues related to hospitalization, and major professional organizations, books, and journals in the field. The information provides an extraordinarily useful guide for learning more about hospital care. Overall, the book draws on vast clinical experience of the authors and pairs this with the latest research. Consequently, the book represents an authoritative, informed, and incisive examination of current residential and inpatient treatments.

—*Alan E. Kazdin, PhD*

PREFACE

Every year, more than 50,000 children and adolescents in the United States receive mental health treatment in residential and inpatient settings. This represents a major investment of personnel and financial resources for our society and subjects the children and families involved to significant disruption of their lives. In light of these monetary and human costs, it is extremely important that the models and methods of treatment used in residential and inpatient settings be scrutinized closely, and that we evaluate the efficacy of these treatment interventions relative to alternative treatment delivery models.

Residential and inpatient care offer tremendous potential for both positive and negative outcomes. No other intervention model can affect all of the elements of a youngster's life to the same extent. This can result in significant and lasting therapeutic change, or it can result in institutionalization and disaffiliation from family and community. This book attempts to provide valuable information to both clinicians and academics regarding the current models and methods of treatment used in residential and inpatient settings. It also attempts to provide guidelines for the use of these services and to suggest alternative models of treatment that may be more cost-effective, more treatment-effective, or both.

In a book of this length, it is impossible to provide comprehensive coverage of all topics relevant to residential and inpatient treatment. Whenever possible, we have provided references to books, book chapters, and journal articles that provide more complete coverage of topics addressed in these pages. We hope that the reference list is among the most useful, and most used, parts of this volume.

We have also attempted in this book to present a historical/chronological view of the field of residential and inpatient treatment. This is a field that has undergone tremendous changes (both philosophical and procedural) in the past 20 years and is still in the process of evolving and defining itself. Only by understanding where we have been in this area can one predict where we will go.

It is our hope that readers of this book can become participants in charting the direction of residential and inpatient treatment in the years to come. We are confronted with the prospect of unprecedented change in the structure of our mental health care delivery system, and serious questions are being asked about all elements of this system. It is our belief that a comprehensive and effective continuum of mental health services for children and adolescents will include residential and inpatient treatment options. Given the expense of these options, however, it is critical that we assess the effectiveness of these treatments and their alternatives objectively and accurately. It is particularly important for research in this area to move to the next level and begin to isolate components of residential and inpatient treatment and investigate their interaction with child and family characteristics and their impact on both short-term and long-term outcome. A simple focus on main effects is no longer sufficient.

We would like to thank a number of individuals for their assistance in this project. Two graduate research assistants, Natalie Hill and Lori Tyler, deserve special thanks for their assistance with the literature research. Two reference librarians also provided much-needed assistance: Kristina Anderson at the University of Alabama Gorgas Library and David Lowe at the University of Alabama Law Center Library. Teri Chisholm, secretary and word-processing genius at Brewer-Porch Children's Center, also deserves special recognition for help in preparing the final manuscript. Nancy Campbell thanks her good friend, Jim Hearn, for his support and, as deadlines loomed, help with many niggling details. Each author thanks the other: Nancy Campbell thanks Bob Lyman for inviting her to participate in the preparation of this book, which has been an invaluable learning experience for her; Bob Lyman thanks Nancy Campbell for her support, feedback, encouragement, and, at times, needed scolding. Finally, we thank the staff and children at Brewer-Porch Children's Center, University of Alabama, for providing the inspiration for, and suggesting much of the content of, this book.

1

MODELS AND ISSUES IN RESIDENTIAL AND INPATIENT TREATMENT

The idea of removing children and adolescents with severe behavioral and emotional disorders from their homes for treatment is an extremely seductive one. Such an action appeals to mental health practitioners because it allows for insulation of the youth from the sometimes countertherapeutic influences of family and community even while it allows for maximization of therapeutic contact and programming.

Such removal needs to be carefully considered prior to implementation, however, because of the potential negative effects of such a placement. Residential and inpatient treatment are invasive interventions. They result in change to virtually every aspect of not only a child's life, but his or her family's as well. Because of the disruptive effects of removing children from their homes and the dangers of institutionalization (Spitz, 1945) and stigmatization that follow, it is important for mental health practitioners to consider all aspects of a clinical situation before making such a treatment recommendation.

Barker (1993) notes a number of both practical and theoretical drawbacks to out-of-home mental health treatment for children and adolescents. He states that the data supporting the effectiveness of residential treatment compared to less invasive interventions are far from conclusive, and he notes that residential treatment can produce institutionalized and overly dependent behavior in children. Barker also states that children and adolescents in residential and inpatient treatment may learn dysfunctional behaviors from other youths in treatment with them. In addition to these problems, which primarily involve the child in treatment, Barker notes that families of children in residential or inpatient treatment may become disengaged from the child while he or she is out of the home, which makes reentering the family system after discharge difficult for the child and decreases the probability of a successful treatment outcome. Finally, Barker acknowledges that residential and inpatient treatment is extremely expensive and may be unavailable to some children in need or a poor choice of limited resources in many cases.

In addition to these practical drawbacks to residential and inpatient mental health treatment for children and adolescents, Barker (1993) also delineates several theoretical objections to the use of such treatment. He points out that children's behavior is highly context dependent and that problem behaviors that are displayed at home or school may often not occur within the context of residential treatment. Conversely, treatment progress achieved within a residential or inpatient treatment environment may not generalize back to home or school.

Barker (1993) also suggests that the diminishing importance of psychoanalytic theory to clinical practice is a theoretical objection to the use of residential and inpatient treatment approaches. Many early residential and inpatient treatment programs were based on a psychoanalytic model that emphasized separation of the child from the pathogenic family environment (Bettelheim, 1974). In recent years, more emphasis has been placed on the treatment of children's mental health problems within the context of the family system (Everett & Volgy, 1993), and such an approach does not encourage removal of the child from the home for treatment. Interestingly, however, the emergence of behaviorism as a major theoretical orientation within mental health has encouraged the development of a new generation of residential and inpatient programs. These programs emphasize the causal role of learning in childhood mental health problems and focus in treatment on the control and manipulation of contingencies in the child's environment. Behaviorists justify using residential and inpatient treatment programs because of the greater environmental control they allow in comparison to outpatient treatment and because of the greater opportunities for direct observation of reinforcement patterns in residential environments. A parallel development to the emergence of behaviorally oriented residential treatment programs has been produced by developments in medicine and psychopharmacology. As medical factors have been identified that contribute to child mental health problems and as effective pharmacological treatments are perfected, there is an increasing need for sophisticated medical diagnostic procedures and complex medication management regimens. Often, these procedures can best be implemented while the child is housed in an inpatient treatment unit.

A final theoretical objection to residential and inpatient treatment that Barker (1993) raises is society's disenchantment with institutional solutions to human problems, resulting in a turn instead to more family-based, community-based, and self-help approaches to such problems. Child mental health approaches consistent with this "new worldview" include individualized interventions involving all family members as full participants in treatment and focusing on preservation of the child's role in the family system. Obviously, such approaches deemphasize the role of residential treatment, particularly if it is long-term and institutional in nature. Intensive, in-home interventions (Kinney, Madsen, Fleming, & Haapala, 1977), day treatment approaches, and the provision of "wrap-around" services (VanDenBerg, 1993) are more consistent with this noninstitutional bias and will be discussed in a later chapter of this book.

Despite acknowledging these drawbacks to the use of residential and inpatient treatment approaches, Barker (1988) does provide several indications for the use of such treatment. He suggests three reasons to consider out-of-home treatment that are directly related to the child's mental health condition. The first of these reasons is when a self-perpetuating cycle of dysfunctional behaviors is well-established, and other, less invasive interventions have proven ineffective. This situation may occur when family dysfunction is a significant causal variable in the child's clinical situation or when such variables as peer reinforcement cannot be controlled in outpatient treatment.

A second indication for residential treatment that is directly related to the child's condition, according to Barker (1993), is when the treatment that the child requires demands technical skills that the parents do not possess and cannot be taught easily. A corollary to this indication is that the treatment needs to be implemented more frequently than can be accommodated in outpatient treatment. A prime example of such an indication for residential treatment is when the child's mental health condition requires a complex, comprehensive behavior management program using components that may be beyond the parents' capabilities.

The third indication for residential treatment cited by Barker (1993) that is directly related to the child's condition is the presence of a psychotic disorder of a magnitude that makes the child unmanageable by parents or other untrained individuals. Although historically, this has been a significant reason for removing children from their homes for treatment, it is noteworthy that several researchers and clinicians (e.g., Lovaas, 1978) have developed models for treating severely disturbed children in the home environment with parents as primary treatment personnel. Outcome data for some of these programs are highly encouraging (Lovaas, 1987).

In addition to these indications for residential treatment that are directly related to the child's clinical condition, Barker (1993) also notes two reasons for considering such treatment that focus primarily on other variables. The first of these is when residential treatment is necessary for the protection of the community. Examples of such circumstances include cases of serious fire-setting or sexual predation in which adequate supervision cannot be ensured without removal from the home.

A second indication for residential treatment that is not directly linked to the child's condition is when removal from the home is necessary for the protection of the child. Examples of situations for which this rationale may be appropriate include suicidal or self-mutilative children for whom home supervision is not adequate to ensure safety, children who run or roam away from home and thus make themselves vulnerable to harm, and children who are at risk for abuse while at home.

Further consideration of the issues involved in removing children and adolescents from their homes for mental health treatment is provided by Lyman, Prentice-Dunn, Wilson, and Taylor (1989). They cite four guiding principles (developed by Wilson & Lyman, 1983) that they believe should govern the decision-making process concerning residential and inpatient care. The first of these principles is that treatment should be provided in the setting that is least disruptive to the child's natural environment but still allows for effective intervention. This requires consideration of the full range of treatment alternatives available in a particular case and an analysis of each alternative's potential treatment effectiveness versus the potential for disruption of the child's life. Such an analysis is not always simple to conduct. Is a month in an inpatient psychiatric ward more disruptive to a child's life than a year in a group home? Which of these alternatives offers the best chance for permanent remediation of the child's (and family's) problems? In conducting such an analysis, it is important that practitioners carefully consider the characteristics of all types of mental health treatment available to them. The major categories of intervention are briefly described below in general order of increasing disruptiveness to the child's natural environment.

CONTINUUM OF CARE

Outpatient Treatment

Outpatient mental health treatment with children and adolescents ranges from verbal psychotherapy (Levitt, 1971) and play therapy (Axline, 1947) to family therapy (Satir, 1967) and behavior therapy (Ross, 1964). It may continue for years or terminate after as few as one or two sessions. Generally, there is little disruption to the child's life. Treatment usually requires a time commitment of no more than 2 or 3 hours per week, and a child's school attendance and community activities are generally minimally affected.

In-Home Interventions

This category of interventions includes those in which mental health practitioners treat the child and/or family in the home environment rather than in an office setting. Because of this intrusion into the home, these interventions generally are more disruptive to the child's natural environment than is outpatient treatment, but they also offer more opportunities for obtaining valuable information about home conditions that may be contributing to the child's disorder and for changing these conditions. The degree to which a mental health practitioner is present in the home varies considerably in these interventions, although usually the interventions are short-term in nature. Examples of such interventions include Lovaas's model of behavioral treatment for autistic children, in which behavioral trainers (as well as parents) implement intensive behavior therapy in the home (Lovaas, 1978); Dry Bed Training for Enuresis (Azrin, Sneed, & Foxx, 1974), in which treatment personnel implement enuresis training procedures for several nights in a child's home; and the Homebuilders model for treating child behavior problems (Kinney et al., 1977), in which a team of mental health practitioners conducts parent training, behavior therapy, and family therapy in a child's home for a period of weeks during crisis periods. These interventions will be discussed in greater depth in a later chapter.

Day Treatment and/or Special Education Programs

These programs offer the advantage of considerably more therapeutic contact with a child than is possible in outpatient treatment without disrupting the child's residential environment. Disadvantages include the ineffectiveness of such programs in addressing behavioral problems that occur primarily in the home environment and the stigmatization and isolation from peers without mental health problems that often occur when a child is placed in a special education program. This stigmatization and isolation may be reduced through the use of "inclusion" or resource programs rather than self-contained class placement (Kirk, 1972), or the use of after-school therapeutic day treatment rather than placement in a special class during school hours.

Shelter or Respite Care

Placement of children in residential or inpatient care for brief periods of time (generally less than 2 weeks) during crisis is usually termed respite care if the purpose is to aid and support parents or other caretakers, and shelter care if the purpose is to protect and treat the child or children in a family. Typically, these two purposes overlap in a given case. Although such an intervention is clearly more invasive than treatment that allows the child to stay in his or her own home, the use of such crisis stabilization techniques is less invasive than long-term removal from the home. Often, the use of respite or shelter care can allow a child to be maintained at home who otherwise would be a candidate for long-term residential treatment.

Foster Care

Removal of a child from home and placement for an extended period of time (1 month to many years) in a foster home with adults who may or may not have received special training in working with children with mental health problems clearly constitutes a major disruption of the child's natural environment. However, some aspects of the child's life may be minimally affected. In most cases, the child will continue to attend public school, possibly even the same school. The foster home environment is "homelike" rather than institutional, and the child is in the care of surrogate parents rather than nursing or child care staff. Typically, there are no more than four or five foster children in a given home. There is usually no explicit treatment "program" in place in foster homes, with the underlying philosophy instead being that exposure to a "good" home environment will ameliorate the child's problems. Therapeutic foster homes—in which foster parents receive specialized training, have professional backup, and generally serve only one foster child—now are being used more often for children with more severe mental health problems in preference to residential treatment, although foster parent burnout and limitations in the public schools' ability to deal with such children are often limiting variables.

Group Home Care

Group home care is differentiated from foster home care by the number of children placed in one home (up to 10 or 12 at a time) and by the degree of structure in the residential environment. Whereas many foster parents act as individual agents, group homes are usually operated as part of child care agencies that employ houseparents, child care workers, social workers, or other staff. Several group homes may be operated by a single agency. Thus, group homes tend to be less homelike and more structured and regimented in their procedures. Although the physical facility often will have the superficial appearance of a family home, other aspects of its operations reveal its agency characteristics. The program typically has an agency name, and an explicit treatment philosophy and program are usually evident in contrast with the more informal provision of treatment by foster parents. Case records are maintained, and frequently, group home "parents" are subordinate to a case supervisor or social worker (a fact that the children in care are well aware of). In most cases, children in group home care attend an external school, although in some agencies, in-house educational programs have been developed. As in foster care, duration of treatment may range from 1 month to a number of years.

Residential Treatment Centers

Programs at residential treatment centers are characterized by stronger agency identification than are group homes and less similarity to children's natural environments. These programs are typically more isolated from the community than are group homes, partially because of a more well-defined "campus" that is less like a family home. More activities for youngsters are provided within the facility rather than in the community. There is almost always a well-defined treatment philosophy and a comprehensive set of procedures by which to implement it. Written treatment plans and comprehensive clinical charts for all children and adolescents are the general rule. Residential treatment programs usually employ treatment staff in addition to houseparents and may use child care workers or nursing staff along with or instead of houseparents for direct care responsibilities. Schooling for at least some youngsters is usually provided at the center. Although the size of such programs may range up to 100 children or more, functional units of no more than 15 children are identified and housed separately. Locked units are in the minority, and the majority of treatment staff typically is made up of nonmedical personnel. The duration of treatment in residential treatment centers may range from several months to a number of years.

Inpatient Hospitalization

The duration of treatment in clearly identified hospital or medically oriented settings is usually shorter (less than 6 months) than for residential treatment centers, but the extreme dissimilarity of the hospital environment to a youngster's natural environment can cause such placements to be more disruptive to a child's or adolescent's life. Typically, nursing staff are used rather than houseparents or child care workers for direct care responsibilities, and there is much more regimentation in daily routines. There is often little opportunity for children or adolescents to engage in such normal activities as room cleaning, snacking, or playing outside. The majority of inpatient child and adolescent psychiatric units are locked, and opportunities for the patients to engage in activities off the unit are usually very limited. Frequently, schooling is suspended temporarily while a child is in the hospital. In other cases, it may be offered on the unit for a brief period each day. Such unfamiliar activities as "rounds," occupational therapy sessions, group therapy, and therapeutic community meetings occupy the rest of the child's day. Meals are often served in a way unfamiliar to children (individual trays prepared in the hospital kitchen and delivered to the unit), and the menu may be unappealing to them. Contacts between the child and his or her parents may be minimal and are often highly structured. Treatment is usually under the direction of a physician, and medication and group, family, or individual psychotherapy are typically considered to be the primary treatment interventions, with the impact of the hospital milieu accorded less significance.

Institutional Treatment

The primary definitional characteristic of institutional programs is the absence of normalizing or natural environmental experiences and a deemphasis on discharge and reentry back into the natural environment. Institutional programs are often physically and attitudinally isolated from the community and rigidly regimented and impersonal in daily routine. Usually, few opportunities are available for residents to leave the facility, and few influences from the community are present within the facility. Generally, the duration of treatment is measured in years. There is little personal freedom given residents in such areas as dress and room decor, and personal possessions are minimal or not easily available to residents. Parental contact is also minimal. Schooling is almost always provided in the institution, and locked units, or the capability of locking residents in their rooms, is a frequent characteristic. Although historically, many state psychiatric hospital child and adolescent psychiatric units have fallen into this category, many have or are currently shedding their institutional characteristics and becoming more like residential treatment centers or inpatient hospital programs. A program of any size, under private or public jurisdiction, may be described as institutional if it does not provide normalizing life experiences for children in care and does not actively pursue the goal of reentry back into the community for its residents.

As stated earlier, a guiding principle in making treatment placement decisions should be the provision of treatment in the environment that is least disruptive to the child's life. Thus, outpatient interventions generally should be considered and/or tried prior to consideration of out-of-home treatment. The appropriate exceptions to this principle are cases requiring immediate out-of-home placement because of danger to the child (or others) or the family's inability to care for him or her, or the need for inpatient hospitalization because of the child's need for intensive medical treatment or diagnosis that cannot be accomplished easily on an outpatient basis. As mentioned earlier, it was thought that certain clinical conditions, such as a severe thought disorder or self-destructive behavior, also suggested the necessity of implementing out-of-home treatment without trying outpatient treatment first. However, research suggests that outpatient management of even severe child and adolescent psychiatric disorders can be safe and highly effective (e.g., Johnson, Whitman, & Barloon-Noble, 1978).

A second principle that Wilson and Lyman (1983) thought should guide treatment placement decisions is that treatment should be provided in the setting that allows for maximum therapeutic efficacy. For example, it would be difficult to treat behavior problems that occur only in a school setting in an inpatient unit that does not have an educational program. Similarly, communication problems between parents and child seldom can be treated effectively if an out-of-home placement minimizes or eliminates parental involvement in treatment. Additionally, it is of critical importance to maximize generalization of treatment effects from the therapeutic environment back to the child's natural environment, and this can be much more difficult to achieve if the therapeutic environment has little in common with the natural environment. It does little good to achieve significant therapeutic progress within residential or inpatient treatment only to see the referral problems reappear upon discharge. Thus, one approach to ensuring that treatment effects generalize as much as possible is to minimize dissimilarities between the therapeutic environment and the environment to which the child will return after treatment (Conway & Bucher, 1976). Treatment programs that are more homelike and school-like offer considerable advantages in this regard and should be considered as preferable treatment options because of the greater probability of effective generalization of treatment effects.

The third principle that Wilson and Lyman (1983) feel should guide treatment placement decisions is that a child's clinical condition and behavior should be matched to the philosophy, structure, and capabilities of the treatment environment. Some children require placement in programs with more resources, such as frequent psychiatric monitoring of medications, awake nighttime staff, or locked facilities, whereas other children can be treated safely and effectively in an unlocked facility with only houseparent supervision at night and no psychiatric consultation. Placement of a child in a program with inadequate resources to treat his or her condition may lead to staff burnout, little or no treatment progress, creation of a nontherapeutic environment for other children in the program, or even circumstances dangerous to the child or others. Conversely, placement of a child in a program with more structure and resources than is necessary to effectively treat the child's clinical condition may result in a loss of treatment effectiveness through decreased generalizability to the home environment, as well as the wasting of limited intensive treatment resources.

Another important aspect of matching a child's needs to a treatment program concerns the fundamental treatment philosophy of a program and the intervention techniques used there. Children with limited verbal abilities and short attention spans are unlikely to get maximum benefit from a program using long-term, psychodynamic psychotherapy as its primary intervention. Similarly, children with problems of depression and anxiety may not derive much benefit from a behavioral treatment program that relies primarily on time-out to reduce acting-out behaviors. Hospital inpatient programs often focus less on educational diagnostics and remediation and thus might be a poor placement choice for treatment of a child with a learning disability resulting in school behavior problems.

MODELS OF RESIDENTIAL TREATMENT

To illustrate the impact of theoretical orientation on treatment characteristics of residential and inpatient programs, six theoretical models of out-of-home treatment and brief descriptions of their basic characteristics will be presented.

The Psychoanalytic Model

Beginning with Aichorn (1935) in the 1930s and continuing with the work of Bettelheim (1950) and Redl and Wineman (1957) in the 1940s and 1950s, psychoanalytic theorists and practitioners postulated a model of residential treatment for children with emotional disorders. One of the basic elements of this model was the isolation of the child from the "psychogenic" influences of the family during treatment (Bettelheim, 1950, 1974). Formal psychodynamic psychotherapy was viewed as the primary therapeutic agent by Bettelheim (1950, 1974), who also discussed ways in which the residential treatment environment could positively and negatively affect children's emotional condition and ways in which this environment could be structured to allow children to explore and resolve their dynamic conflicts. Redl (1966), in contrast to Bettelheim, emphasized the primary role of treatment by child care workers in the residential environment through the "life space interview," a set of verbal interventions initiated by staff in response to events occurring in the child's daily life. These interventions were psychoanalytically based but expressed in practical terms and intended for use by houseparents, nurses, and paraprofessionals.

Redl's work, however, conflicts with the child guidance model, which represents the mainstream of analytically based residential treatment today (Whittaker, 1979). This model emphasizes the importance of formal psychotherapy as the primary therapeutic intervention and generally relegates the efforts of nursing and child care staff to secondary status. Such programs, however, generally have not presented much data in support of their effectiveness, and they appear to be less appropriate than behaviorally oriented programs for children with limited intellectual or verbal abilities, nonmiddle-class backgrounds, or behavioral disorders that appear to result primarily from maladaptive social learning.

The Behavioral Model

Residential treatment programs based on the principles of learning theory developed as part of the general emergence of behavior therapy as a major treatment model in the 1960s and 1970s. The psychoanalytic model had been dominant throughout the first half of the 20th century, but its limited applicability to some client populations (retarded, psychotic, nonverbal) and the lack of empirical demonstration of its treatment effectiveness encouraged a search for alternative treatment approaches.

This search led to the application of laboratory-derived learning principles to the treatment of human psychological problems. Wolpe (1958) produced the first widely distributed and accepted work in support of behavior therapy, and Lazarus (1960), Ferster (1961), Ross (1964), and Lovaas, Freitag, Nelson, and Whalen (1967), among others, extended the use of these techniques into the area of child therapy. Soon, models for behaviorally based residential treatment of children's emotional and behavioral problems were also in place.

Such behaviorally oriented residential treatment programs share a focus on the child's overt behavior rather than on such covert elements as inner personality states or dynamic conflicts. Maladaptive behaviors are viewed as largely resulting from past learning experiences. Remediation of these behaviors usually consists of systematic management of positive and negative consequences in the residential environment or control of stimulus-response pairings in accordance with established learning principles. On-line child care workers, because of their role in managing the treatment environment, are often viewed as the primary treatment agents, as opposed to the child guidance model's view of the psychiatric team as central in importance. Behavioral treatment programs have generated tremendous quantities of data in support of their treatment effectiveness over the past 25 years. Such programs appear to be effective with a broad range of problem behaviors, including such clinical conditions as anorexia, autism, attention-deficit disorder, conduct disorder, phobias, enuresis, encopresis, and others. Behavioral programs also appear to be more applicable than psychoanalytic programs to children with poor verbal and intellectual abilities. A number of comprehensive models for behaviorally based residential treatment exist, including those developed at Achievement Place (Phillips, Phillips, Wolf, & Fixsen, 1973), the National Training School (Cohen & Filipczak, 1971), and the Children's Center of Wisconsin (Browning & Stover, 1971). The Teaching-Family Model, which derived from work at Achievement Place and is currently the model espoused by the Boy's Town network of facilities, may be the most dominant current example of behaviorally based residential care (Blase, Fixsen, Freeborn, & Jaeger, 1989).

The Medical Inpatient Model

Since the first children's psychiatric inpatient units were established, such as the one begun in the pediatric department of Johns Hopkins Hospital in 1930 (Freedman, Kaplan, & Sadock, 1972), there has been a tremendous increase in the number of such programs. Although initially there was a strong psychoanalytic orientation to these units, in recent years, many have become more eclectic and "medicalized," with a strong emphasis on medical diagnosis and interventions. The types of cases that appear to be most effectively treated in psychiatric inpatient units are those with organic causalities or those for whom somatic treatments are most effective. Given the limited duration of most inpatient psychiatric hospitalizations, long-term interventions are not feasible. As pointed out earlier, inpatient units frequently do not offer effective environments for dealing with school or family problems because of the deemphasis on educational programming and the limited contact between the child patient and his or her family. The inpatient unit staff is also usually more familiar, because of training and experience, with medical diagnosis and treatment and may emphasize organic causal explanations and treatments over educational and psychosocial ones. A growing role for psychiatric inpatient units is periodic hospitalization of chronically mentally ill children and adolescents, including those with mental retardation, autism, and thought or conduct disorders, for the purpose of stabilizing behavior and providing respite to the family. Additionally, as medical diagnostic procedures in the area of mental health become more sophisticated and important, psychiatric inpatient units increasingly will become a place where children are housed while such diagnostic procedures as MRIs, CT and PET scans, sleep EEGs, and laboratory assays are conducted. One factor that may work against increased use of psychiatric inpatient units in an era of managed care is their cost. Psychiatric inpatient care generally costs between $500 and $1,000 per day, whereas other varieties of out-of-home care for mentally ill children and adolescents generally cost between $50 and $300 per day.

The Psychoeducational Model

The psychoeducational model is a variant of the behavioral model and is best represented by Project Re-Ed in Tennessee (Hobbs, 1966). Like the behavioral model, it stresses the teaching of more appropriate behaviors and coping skills to children and adolescents. A fundamental part of the psychoeducational model is an emphasis on community involvement and continued contact between a child and his or her family, if at all possible. As a result, psychoeducational programs appear to be particularly effective in promoting generalization of treatment effects to the home environment. Like behavioral programs, psychoeducational programs appear to have applicability to a broad range of client types and clinical conditions. Like other behavioral programs, they also emphasize the importance of on-line staff, the structuring of daily activities, and the management of positive and negative consequences in the residential environment rather than verbal psychotherapy.

The Peer Culture Model

The peer culture model stresses the importance of interpersonal factors in residential therapeutic programming. Raush, Dittman, and Taylor (1959) and Polsky (1962) were among the first to formally recognize what had long been informally known; that peer influences are often of far more significance to a child in residential treatment than the therapeutic efforts of staff. Following this recognition, a number of authors, including Flackett and Flackett (1970) and Vorrath and Brendtro (1974), offered formal treatment approaches intended to enlist peer support for positive rather than negative behavioral change in residential treatment.

Most peer culture programs rely on formal or informal group discussions of resident behavior as well as some degree of group control over individuals' privileges or rewards. The effectiveness of the treatment derives from both the confrontation and feedback of the group discussions and the reinforcement of appropriate behavior with positive consequences. Staff members are significantly involved as participants in the group process, but much of the effectiveness of these programs can be attributed to interactions between residents.

The peer culture model (often described as "therapeutic community") has become the model of choice for inpatient adolescent programs, particularly in the area of substance abuse. This is a logical development because many substance abuse problems appear to be related to peer pressure. Other externalizing disorders also appear to be amenable to treatment via the peer culture model, whereas more internalized disorders appear less appropriate for such an intervention. The peer culture model requires a fairly high level of intellectual and verbal ability for optimal participation and is not suited for use with mentally retarded children, those with serious psychotic disorders, or very young children. It is imperative that staff working within a peer culture model program realize that they must exert considerable guidance and control over group discussions and decisions to avoid nontherapeutic excesses or punitive actions.

The Wilderness Therapy Model

Camping and contact with nature have been assumed to be therapeutic for children much longer than they have been formally associated with the mental health establishment. The first camps with a consciously therapeutic focus were those developed in the 1920s and 1930s to benefit underprivileged urban youngsters (McNeil, 1962). By the mid-1930s, camps were being developed with a formal mental health focus rather than the more general goal of providing structured and supervised recreation in a healthful outdoor setting (Young, 1939).

In subsequent years, there have been two different thrusts to the development of outdoor therapeutic programs. On one hand, a wide range of camping programs has emerged that use traditional group and individual therapy techniques to treat children in a camp setting. Many of these programs are time-limited (usually summer) extensions of year-round residential treatment programs. Others are free-standing and may operate just during the summer or may operate all year in a camp setting. The duration of the camp experience for an individual child may vary from a week or less to a year or more, and activities usually include traditional camp recreation along with more specifically therapeutic experiences. A fairly recent development has been the use of a camp environment to address the psychosocial consequences of such chronic childhood medical conditions as diabetes, obesity, and cancer (Harkavy et al., 1983). Therapeutic camping programs may range in theoretical orientation from behavioral to psychodynamic. There are a number of published studies suggesting that such programs offer a cost- and treatment-effective approach to childhood emotional disturbance (e.g., Ploufe, 1981; Rickard & Dinoff, 1974). A particular advantage to such programs is that they offer an opportunity for intense out-of-home treatment without the disadvantages of stigmatization and institutionalization that sometimes accompany more traditional residential treatment.

Wilderness therapy programs, the second thrust in outdoor therapeutic programming, are derived primarily from the Outward Bound model originated by Kurt Hahn (Richards, 1981). These programs attempt to offer challenging, transcendent experiences in the wilderness that will call forth prosocial values and behavior in children and adolescents. Wilderness therapy programs are primarily group centered and offer challenges to comfort and safety that, when successfully dealt with, may provide a new repertoire of coping skills and enhanced self-esteem for the participants. In addition, new ways of relating to others are explored. The challenges offered can range from hiking and mountain climbing to sailing or living off the land. Some programs use specific missions such as building a cabin or making a cross-country trek in covered wagons. A number of research studies have documented the impact of these interventions (e.g., Freeman, Spilka, & Mason, 1968; Gibson, 1981). One caution concerning these programs is the need to ensure that challenges are offered in a physically and psychologically safe environment. Sometimes, inadequately trained or misguided staff may overdo the rigor of physical challenges or treat noncompliance of participants in a punitive, nonsupportive way. This is a violation of the original philosophy of such programs.

PROGRAM CHARACTERISTICS

Although there are major theoretical and philosophical differences among these treatment models, there are also a number of more practical considerations that must be addressed by any residential program that are guided only partly by theory. These program characteristics can determine the nature and therapeutic effectiveness of any residential or inpatient program, regardless of theoretical orientation. Some of these variables are discussed below.

Physical Facilities

A program's physical characteristics are determined to some degree by theoretical considerations but even more so by such practical considerations as availability of funds, community acceptance, accreditation criteria, and zoning laws. Attention to physical facilities varies in the residential treatment literature, with Bettelheim, for example, discussing at length the importance of the appearance of bathrooms in assisting children in working through problems associated with the anal stage of psychosexual development (Bettelheim & Sanders, 1979). Most other authorities, however, devote little time to addressing the issue of physical facilities. Many treatment programs use converted homes as residences with relatively few modifications; others use specially constructed buildings with such features as childproof windows and secure time-out rooms. There are also significant differences between treatment programs in the amount of personal space and privacy allowed children as well as in the amount and ease of access to the community.

Although these appear to be important variables in determining the milieu to which a child is subjected, there are no empirical studies in the research literature to guide the design of physical facilities. A critical concern already discussed is enhancement of treatment generalization and ease of reentry back into the community following residential treatment. These factors would suggest that more homelike, community-based physical facilities would be preferable to more institutional buildings and grounds, but little research has been done to support this conclusion.

Staffing

Staffing is considered to be a critical issue in every residential treatment program, but there are considerable differences of opinion as to optimal staffing configurations and which staff members are considered primary to treatment. The traditional view of the child's psychotherapist as the central figure in treatment, with the on-line staff considered secondary and part of the "other 23 hours" (Trieschman, Whittaker, &

Brendtro, 1969), has, to some extent, given way to the recognition that all members of the milieu are important. This may be due, in part, to the practical reality that psychologists, psychiatrists, and social workers rarely spend more than a brief period of time each day with each child in residential treatment.

Residential programs vary widely in how much attention is given to the selection, training, and supervision of paraprofessional staff and in how involved such individuals are in treatment planning and implementation. As mentioned earlier, programs also vary in whether on-line staff are nurses, child care workers, or houseparents. Advantages and disadvantages can be cited for each staffing model, but there is little empirical evidence supporting these arguments.

Characteristics of Children Served

Most residential and inpatient programs have stated eligibility criteria, with particular behavioral or emotional problems targeted that are assumed to be most responsive to the treatment offered by the program. These tend to be rather vague (e.g., "school behavior problems" or "authority problems") and are seldom based upon a review of the program's outcome data. Programs are usually much more specific regarding exclusion criteria (i.e., the types of children or problems that are considered inappropriate for admission, such as firesetters or suicidal adolescents). Unfortunately, these criteria are more often based upon liability concerns or staff anxiety than on an objective appraisal of the program's capabilities.

It is misleading to focus entirely on the behavior of the child as the only criterion for admission to residential or inpatient treatment. As mentioned in the first part of this chapter, it is important to examine other factors, such as the community's tolerance for particular behaviors, the range of alternative services available, and the willingness and ability of parents and school personnel to work with and manage the child's behavior. Residential treatment is often necessitated because of an inadequate fit between the treatment needs of the child and the resources available in the child's natural environment. Although primarily focusing on the child, residential treatment programs should also attend explicitly to these other factors, for example, by conducting parent training and various forms of community education.

Involvement of the Child in Treatment

There is wide variation in how much or in what ways children are involved in their treatment in residential and inpatient settings. Some programs exclude not only the child but also the entire family from active involvement in treatment planning and implementation. Others specifically provide for such involvement in their treatment procedures. For instance, peer culture programs require that children be major participants in determining their own treatment goals and in evaluating progress (Vorrath & Brendtro, 1974). Behaviorally oriented programs also have often provided for client involvement, with techniques including self-monitoring procedures, behavioral contracting, and goal-setting and self-control training (e.g., Lyman, 1984; Stuart, 1971). Points and levels systems also may be used in ways that can either encourage or undermine personal involvement and responsibility (Kazdin, 1977). Some residential programs even allow children to attend treatment planning meetings and participate in writing their own treatment plan (Dinoff, Rickard, Love, & Elder, 1978).

The Role of Psychotherapy

In the past, psychotherapy was often seen as the main instrument of therapeutic change in residential and inpatient treatment, with the rest of the program serving only to house the children and insulate them from countertherapeutic influences. Today, however, residential programs in which formal psychotherapy is considered the primary agent of change are in the minority. "A truly therapeutic milieu cannot be organized around the concept of individual psychotherapy as the central mode of treatment" (Whittaker, 1979, p. 56).

What exactly should the role of psychotherapy be? Results of research in child psychotherapy are equivocal (Weisz & Weiss, 1993) and suggest that verbal psychotherapy should not be the treatment of choice for many children. In addition, psychotherapy within the context of residential or inpatient settings is subject to very different influences and expectations than is outpatient psychotherapy. Children may be referred for psychotherapy mainly when they are behaving badly, with the therapy viewed merely as an extension of the program's behavior management system. Also, there are a number of questions concerning confidentiality and client advocacy that must be addressed when a child is seen in psychotherapy within the context of residential or inpatient treatment.

The Role of the Group

Regardless of the stated theoretical orientation upon which a residential or inpatient program is based, much of what happens to a child in treatment will be determined by group interactions and influences. Much power resides in the peer subculture that develops in residential treatment (Polsky, 1962; Polsky & Claster, 1968), and peers frequently reinforce undesirable behaviors (Buehler, Patterson, & Furniss, 1966). The peer culture model discussed earlier attempts to explicitly use peer influences as a therapeutic force (Vorrath & Brendtro, 1974), whereas some behavioral programs such as Achievement Place have attended to these influences through the use of such techniques as peer managers and peer monitoring (Phillips, Phillips, Fixsen, & Wolf, 1971).

Other ways to make the group a therapeutic agent include the use of group problem-solving methods (Loughmiller, 1965), the use of group contingencies and reinforcement (Herman & Tramontana, 1971), and reliance on formal group therapy. Another important consideration in harnessing the group as a therapeutic influence is the composition of the group of children in residential treatment at any given time, with too high a proportion of children with externalizing problems making it difficult to create a positive peer culture (Redl, 1966).

Specific Skill Training

The learning of adaptive behaviors, such as self-help, prosocial, and academic skills, is an important component of many residential and inpatient treatment programs. Project Re-Ed (Hobbs, 1966), for example, "stresses the teaching of competence across the total spectrum of the child's development as the fundamental purpose of the helping environment" (Whittaker, 1979, p. 71). Behavioral programs, such as Achievement Place, also have taken note of the importance of specific skills training, with the learning of adaptive behaviors often an explicit goal for children in treatment.

Specific intervention techniques that often have been used to teach adaptive skills include social skills training (Clark, Caldwell, & Christian, 1979), structured modeling by staff and other group members (Rogers-Warren & Baer, 1976), and contingency management applied to academic performance (Rickard & Dinoff, 1974).

Behavior Management and Control

Even residential and inpatient programs that consider psychotherapy as the primary therapeutic agent must attend to issues of behavioral control and management. Approaches to this issue range from the permissive tolerance for inappropriate behavior seen at the psychodynamically oriented Orthogenic School (Bettelheim, 1974) to the highly structured interventions implemented at many behaviorally oriented programs. The writings of Redl (1966) can be considered a blend of psychoanalytical philosophy and behavioral practicalities in dealing with issues of control and management. *The Other 23 Hours* (Trieschman et al., 1969) also contains a number of chapters addressing the issue of managing problem behaviors in residential treatment.

Behaviorally oriented programs have attended most explicitly to issues of and techniques for behavior management and control. A number of behavioral techniques with documented efficacy are directly applicable in residential treatment. These include such interventions as points and levels systems (Kazdin, 1977), overcorrection techniques (Azrin & Wesolowski, 1974), behavioral contracting (Stuart, 1971), self-control training (Drabman, Spitalnik, & O'Leary, 1973) and time-out procedures (Wilson & Lyman, 1982). Browning and Stover (1971) and Monkman (1972), among others, provide detailed descriptions of the use of behavioral interventions in residential treatment.

The limitations of behavior management and control techniques also should be recognized. The ultimate purpose of residential and inpatient treatment is to improve functioning in the home environment, not merely control behavior in the residential treatment setting. These techniques are truly effective only when they are part of a comprehensive program for teaching children more adaptive skills to enable them to live better in the less structured environment of their homes and communities.

Parental Involvement in Treatment

Involving parents in their child's residential treatment is often problematic because the child is away from home, with treatment staff assuming many of what are usually parental functions. Separation from parents is also, at times, considered to be therapeutic for children, especially in cases in which the parents are viewed as at least partially responsible for their child's emotional and behavioral problems. Despite these difficulties, most residential and inpatient treatment providers would agree that treatment success is, to a large extent, dependent on meaningful and sustained involvement of parents (or other caretakers) in the treatment process, and that the child and family both should be regarded as clients.

Geographic factors, parents' emotional problems, feelings of guilt and failure because of their child's placement, or lack of encouragement on the part of the residential facility all may be factors that inhibit parental involvement. In addition, increasing numbers of children in residential and inpatient settings lack functional or identifiable parents and/or are in agency custody, making family involvement unlikely. Techniques to increase family involvement include offering parent support groups, providing parent education, and specific skills training classes, and encouraging parents to attend and conducting family therapy sessions. At times, involvement of the parents in nontherapeutic recreational activities at the residential facility can open the door to increased therapeutic involvement. Whatever philosophy intervention is based on, research indicates that for treatment to be successful, change must occur in the child's home environment as well as in the child (Taylor & Alpert, 1973). Treatment of the child without involvement of the parents is unlikely to produce meaningful and long-lasting remediation.

Community Linkages

Although residential care, by definition, involves some disruption of a child's life, it is imperative that as much continuity and communication as possible be maintained between the residential treatment environment and the child's home environment. Preparing for discharge and seeking to enhance treatment generalization should be a continuing concern throughout treatment (Conway & Bucher, 1976). There should be provisions for a child to have regular interactions with his or her home environment while in residential care through home visits, placement in community schools if possible, and parent involvement in family therapy. Only rarely is a residential treatment program justified in severing all contacts between a child and his or her home environment. At times, it may be necessary for the residential program to create "artificial" community linkages for a child who otherwise would not have them. The use of "visiting resources" such as short-term foster homes can create a degree of community involvement for the child.

Residential staff may be willing to provide community experiences in their own homes for children without other resources. There also should be linkages between the residential treatment program and the child's home environment after discharge. The support and guidance of residential treatment staff can be critical in determining the success of the posttreatment placement.

Community linkages are also critical at the agency level. To ensure community receptivity to the residential program's mission and to guarantee access to community resources, a high level of communication must be maintained. Coates and Miller (1972) describe some of the community liaison problems that confront residential treatment programs. These range from neighbors' fears of residents' behavior to concerns that property values near the facility will suffer. The most effective way to combat such attitudes is by open communication between residential program staff and community residents.

The issues discussed above are ones that must be addressed within any residential or inpatient program. Often, the approaches taken in dealing with these issues will determine the nature and effectiveness of the program far more than its treatment philosophy.

COST EFFECTIVENESS

The last principle listed by Wilson and Lyman (1983) in their consideration of residential treatment is that care should be implemented in as cost effective a manner as possible. Clearly, one component in an analysis of cost effectiveness is treatment effectiveness. An intervention cannot be viewed as cost effective (even if it is very inexpensive) if it does not produce the desired result. The issue of the efficacy of residential and inpatient treatment will be addressed in a later chapter of this volume.

An adequate appraisal of cost effectiveness must also include consideration of such variables as treatment duration and the social and human cost of treatment failure. Five years of weekly outpatient therapy at $100 per hour or no treatment at all may prove far more costly than 6 months of residential treatment at $200 per day if the above factors are adequately considered. Cost effectiveness also needs to be considered in comparing different types of residential and inpatient care. For example, if a therapeutic camp program can treat a child effectively for $50 per day, is there any justification for using residential care in a more traditional setting at $200 per day? In this context, such alternatives as day treatment and in-home treatment (discussed in a later chapter) need to be considered carefully. The question of cost effectiveness is becoming increasingly important in an era of managed care, decreasing governmental support for human services, and increased accountability.

SUMMARY

There are drawbacks and limitations, as well as advantages, to the use of residential and inpatient approaches to the treatment of child and adolescent emotional and behavioral disorders. These drawbacks include the somewhat equivocal evidence for the effectiveness of such treatment, the disruption of family relationships that may occur, and the potential for learning maladaptive behaviors by children in treatment through modeling by other residents. The advantages include the degree of behavioral and environmental control that can be achieved, the amount of therapeutic programming that can be delivered, and the insulation from negative environmental influences that is provided.

A consideration of residential and inpatient treatment also requires careful consideration of the alternatives to such treatment that are available. These alternatives span a continuum from outpatient psychotherapy to institutionalization, with each treatment mode having differential applicability to individual cases. There are several principles that should guide the consideration of these treatment alternatives. These principles include the provision of treatment within the setting least disruptive to the child's life, use of a treatment setting that maximizes treatment efficacy and generalizability, and consideration of cost-effectiveness.

A residential or inpatient treatment program's theoretical orientation clearly influences its methodology and effectiveness. Six theoretical models of treatment (e.g., psychoanalytic, behavioral, medical inpatient, psychoeducational, peer culture, and wilderness therapy) are represented among residential and inpatient providers. The structure, activities, target populations, and effectiveness of these programs vary widely. In addition, such nontheoretical variables as physical facilities, staffing patterns, parent involvement, and community integration also affect the nature of residential and inpatient treatment programs. A careful consideration of residential and inpatient program characteristics, treatment alternatives, and client needs is necessary to optimize treatment outcome.

2

THE CLIENTS: ADMISSIONS AND TREATMENT PLANNING

Four approaches to establishing admission criteria for children's and adolescents' mental health services have been identified by Friedman and Street (1985): "(a) the use of general principles or standards, (b) the reliance on expert judgment, (c) the experimental and empirical approach, and (d) the case study approach" (p. 231). Traditionally, in both inpatient and residential settings, experts have made admission decisions guided by their professional training in mental health and by relevant public policy, legal, and financial considerations. Currently, such "general principles" in the field encourage social service agencies and mental health professionals to provide services in cost-effective, least restrictive settings—ideally local, community-based, family-focused treatment programs that are part of a continuum of care or system of services that can accommodate a wide range of mental health needs (e.g., Duchnowski & Friedman, 1990; Lewis & Summerville, 1991; Tuma, 1989; Wells, 1991; Wilson & Lyman, 1983). Inpatient and residential treatment programs are increasingly expected to articulate and demonstrate their unique positions on the continuum of care, so that referrals to them may be justified and appropriate (Jemerin & Phillips, 1988; Lane, 1993).

Inpatient settings include public and private psychiatric hospitals, children's hospitals or children's units within general hospitals, psychiatric units of general hospitals, and chemical dependency programs. The most expensive form of treatment, inpatient treatment is also usually considered the most intensive, restrictive, and secure. Inpatient programs serve seriously emotionally or behaviorally disturbed youths who require a secure facility, often in emergency situations when the prospective patient poses an immediate intentional or unintentional threat to self or others.[1] Patients may be suicidal or assaultive, or they may be prone to harming themselves or others accidentally because of extreme impulsivity or impaired judgment (e.g., while intoxicated or psychotic). Inpatient settings allow for the initiation and monitoring of psychotropic medication and accommodate children with medical as well as psychiatric disorders (Gadpaille, 1985; Hendren, 1991; Jemerin & Phillips, 1988; Miller & Burt, 1982; Tuma, 1989; Woolston, 1991).

The psychiatric diagnoses given child and adolescent inpatients cover the gamut of known disorders, but the preponderance are those associated with dangerous acting-out, conditions that are frequently comorbid with such acting-out, and serious psychopathology (Cornsweet, 1990). Bereika and Mikkelsen (1992) summarized five studies of inpatients' diagnoses by concluding that the most common were those involving mood disorders or disruptive behaviors; two of the studies also reported significant numbers of adjustment disorders. Another short-term psychiatric unit's records revealed that, over a 2-year period, behavioral problems, mood disturbances, and psychoses comprised the majority of their child patients' diagnoses; nearly half of the children carried multiple diagnoses (Dalton, Bolding, Woods, & Daruna, 1987). Pfeffer, Plutchik, and Mizruchi's (1986) comparison of child psychiatric inpatients with outpatients and nonpatients indicated that inpatients were more severely disturbed than the other two groups, and outpatients more so than nonpatients. Inpatients exhibited more suicidal, aggressive, and depressive behaviors; they had the poorest reality testing and impulse control; and they were most likely to use defenses of projection and regression. Inpatients were also most likely to have diagnoses of conduct disorder, schizophrenia, organic brain syndrome, or pervasive developmental disorder. Presumably, adolescent inpatients would be diagnosed more frequently than child inpatients with schizophrenia, substance abuse, or anorexia nervosa, as well as other disorders with a typically older age of onset (American Psychiatric Association, 1994; Gadpaille, 1985).

There appear to be no empirical comparisons of youths admitted to inpatient as opposed to residential treatment programs, but there are a few comparisons of children in residential treatment with those receiving nonresidential services. A study of 812 children and adolescents in either residential treatment or special education programs in school settings across four different states demonstrated that the two groups differed in clinical presentation and background variables (Silver et al., 1992). Clinically, residents were more likely than special education students to be diagnosed with attention deficit disorder, conduct disorder, or anxiety; more likely to have received psychotropic medications; and more likely to be rated by parents as exhibiting higher levels of internalizing as well as externalizing behaviors. Teacher ratings of their behavior were ambiguous: On one measure, teachers rated residents as more often exhibiting conduct problems, but on another measure, teachers rated residents as exhibiting more serious internalizing behaviors. Residents also exhibited poorer adaptive behaviors, were more self-derogating, and self-reported more serious behavior problems.

On familial variables, residents in treatment were less likely than special education students to have lived with two biological parents and more likely to come from "blended" families. They were also more likely to have come from low-income households; to have previously lived in a foster home, group home, or institution; to have abuse mentioned in their records; to have received child welfare investigation services; and to have had a social agency other than school provide their first assistance. The two groups were similar in intelligence (average measured IQ of 86, with standard deviation of 16.9), reading and math achievement (below grade level), and age of onset of problem (mean age of 5 years, 10 months for boys and 7 years, 1 month for girls).

An examination of the variables predictive of children's and preadolescents' placement in more or less restrictive residential settings (e.g., highly structured institutions rather than group homes) demonstrated that less restrictive placements were associated with children having primarily family problems, whereas more restrictive placements were associated with children exhibiting problems themselves (Pierce, 1985). However, not all studies have demonstrated significant clinical differences between children placed in residential treatment settings and less restrictive settings. For example, a comparison of youngsters ages 6 to 16 years old in either day treatment or residential treatment did not find many clinical differences in the two groups; they differed primarily by "locale of residence" (Prentice-Dunn, Wilson, & Lyman, 1981).

Most empirical studies of children and adolescents in residential treatment have been descriptive rather than comparative, and the majority have generated similar descriptions of youths in residential treatment. Residents not only typically present with significant, chronic emotional or behavioral problems, but they also come to treatment centers with a host of demographic and background variables suggestive of family instability and dysfunction. In a recent study, Wells and Whittington (1993) studied all nonpsychotic, nonmentally retarded youths, ages 10 to 17 years old, referred to a residential treatment facility during the course of a year by interviewing parents or other adults well-acquainted with each youth and administering several behavioral and family inventories. Half of the youths were in the custody of a county department of human services, and the majority had not seen one or the other of their biological parents in more than a year. On standardized behavior rating scales, they exhibited a high frequency of clinically significant behavior problems and low social competency. Almost half were viewed as having been in crisis for more than 6 months, and 96% previously had used some sort of mental health, welfare, juvenile justice, or emergency shelter service. These youths differed significantly from their siblings on two measures: academic competence and social competence. More than half of the study youths had been enrolled in a class for the learning disabled and/or behaviorally disordered, and almost half had repeated at least one grade. The majority of families studied reported low-income, moderate stress, abuse-related concerns, as well as reticence about their child living at home. They were more likely than nonclinical families providing normative data to report interactional styles at the extremes on measures of cohesion and flexibility/rigidity. Despite the high rate of difficulties identified in the study, the investigators did discover considerable variability among the youths and their families; substantial numbers scored in nonclinical ranges on the various measures employed.

Cates's (1991) review of the characteristics of children referred during the 1980s to residential treatment indicated that the preschool children clustered into two groups: autistic children and children who shared a common set of familial characteristics (e.g., multiple foster home placements, biological father absent from home of origin, biological mother experiencing a major psychiatric disorder).[2] Children in the latter group typically exhibited conduct disorders, although other diagnoses were also represented. In his analysis of studies including older children, Cates (1991) concluded that family dysfunction had preceded, and probably predisposed, these children's referrals for residential treatment as well.

In a review of demographic variables and clinical ratings characterizing comparable samples of child and adolescent residents of the Sonia Shankman Orthogenic School of the University of Chicago at the beginning of each of five decades, spanning 1950 through 1990, Zimmerman (1994) identified trends in residents' funding sources as well as their personal and family characteristics. In 1990, all students were supported by public funds, in contrast to the funding of students in the 1950s and 1960s primarily by their generally middle- to upper middle-class families, supplemented by contributions from private charities. The majority of residents had come from intact families with both biological parents in the 1950s through the 1970s; by 1990, only 20% had such intact families, and 40% were wards of the state. Socioeconomic status had decreased significantly as well. Average age and prior education completed fluctuated over time but increased overall, and recent residents are more racially diverse. Clinically, residents had been diagnosed primarily as psychotic until the present decade; in 1990, residents typically had multiple diagnoses, with conduct disorder, depression, attention deficit, and hyperactivity occurring most often. Almost one third exhibited symptoms of posttraumatic stress disorder; 40% had histories of prior physical, ritual, or sexual abuse. These residents also had more changes in living arrangements than did earlier residents, as well as more unsuccessful previous treatment attempts. Across the five decades, residents exhibited significant psychopathology (primarily process rather than reactive in nature) and impaired functioning, with an early age of onset (mean of 5.18 years).

A study of 211 child and adolescent residents (ages 7 to 20 years) in 15 treatment-oriented group homes and residential treatment centers in Alabama in the early 1980s revealed patterns similar to those cited above (Wurtele, Wilson, & Prentice-Dunn, 1983). Residents were typically referred for externalizing behaviors (including noncompliance and aggression), immaturity, and poor academic achievement. Few came from intact families; prior to admission, their residences had included detention centers, shelter care, group homes, foster families, adoptive families, institutions (including other residential treatment facilities), and one or the other or both of their biological parents. The majority had experienced three or more changes in their living arrangements. Comparisons of the child and adolescent residents revealed less hyperactivity and more substance abuse, delinquent behaviors, sexual acting-out, anxiety, immaturity, and academic problems among the adolescents. Some sex differences were observed as well. Other reports (Sunday & Moore, 1988, in Cates, 1991; Whittaker, Fine, & Grasso, 1989) on adolescents in residential treatment have indicated that males in group home and residential treatment settings are often delinquent (or conduct disordered), immature, withdrawn, and hyperactive. Females in group homes are described as conduct disordered as well, and females in residential centers have been rated as conduct disordered or exhibiting other symptomatic behavior, including anxiety and hyperactivity.

In summary, the contemporary population of youths being admitted into residential treatment is characterized by chronic, multiple problem behaviors that have not responded well to previous treatment attempts—especially disruptive behavior disorders, depression, and posttraumatic stress disorder. The youngsters appear to have significant skills deficits, such as in academic achievement and social competency. Their families appear to be significantly dysfunctional and unstable, as reflected, for example, in high rates of abuse concerns and family dissolution. This picture of the current population in residential treatment is consistent with criteria for admission proposed by the National Association of Psychiatric Treatment Centers for Children (1990; in Wells, 1991):

> A . . . diagnosis which indicates the presence of a mental disorder which is moderate to severe in nature and is not a transient reactive disorder; the impairment of functioning in at least one of the following: family, vocation/school, community; an acute disturbance of affect, behavior or thinking; the potential of danger to self or others; the need for continuous, comprehensive, holistic treatment; the therapeutic potential to benefit from the program and be transferred to outpatient care within a predictable time as established by a treatment and discharge plan. (p. 342)

The possible benefits of residential treatment for such youngsters include protection for those who have been abused, who are self-injurious or suicidal, or who place themselves in dangerous situations. Residential treatment also affords protection to the youth's family, peers, and others in the community who might be the targets of dangerous acting-out. Residential placement may also allow for assessment not possible in other settings, particularly isolating the contributions of environmental variables to a youngster's disturbance. However, probably the most distinctive benefit of residential treatment, rather than simply residential placement, is the stability it provides children and adolescents who come from chaotic or otherwise seriously dysfunctional backgrounds, whose development is seriously impaired so they are immature and have poor internal controls, and who have not responded adequately to treatment in less restrictive settings. The treatment setting should provide a continuously therapeutic environment and enduring relationships that augment the more specific therapies provided (Barker, 1982, 1993; Kaplan & Sadock, 1985; Lewis & Summerville, 1991; Thomas, 1989; Wurtele et al., 1983).

ADMISSION AND TREATMENT PLANNING

Children and adolescents are often admitted to a psychiatric hospital or other inpatient setting on short notice to staff because of emergency precipitating events. Prospective patients and their parents or guardians may present themselves for the admission with little, if any, notice, although many are referred by mental health professionals. Referrals to residential treatment are usually more protracted, although emergency referrals may be made. Typically initiated by mental health professionals or staff of social service agencies, the referrals usually provide considerable background information for residential staff to review before a prospective resident is seen for intake (Kaplan & Sadock, 1985; Lewis & Summerville, 1991).

In both settings, an intake assessment is typically conducted by observation and interview. It usually includes evaluation of the youth's current mental status, the precipitating events leading up to the admission, and relevant background information that helps establish whether admission is appropriate and aids treatment planning (Hendren, 1991). Particulars discussed include the youth's presenting problems, psychiatric and educational histories, developmental and family background, and strengths. Family, referring professionals, and the prospective client often contribute to the assessment. Goals include understanding the youngster's immediate and longer term treatment needs within the larger context of family and community.

Admission is a two-part process, one part helping staff anticipate a new resident's treatment needs, the other part helping the client make the transition into treatment (Swanson & Schaefer, 1993). The youngster should have been prepared for admission by family and referral sources explaining when and where he or she is going, and why. They, along with program staff, can help the child or adolescent anticipate what the inpatient or residential stay will be like by describing the program and answering questions. Ideally, preplacement visits help ease the transition for youngsters entering residential treatment. If not, at admission they should be given a tour that includes seeing the resident's bedroom, cottage, and classroom and meeting staff and other residents. Therapists should meet their clients soon to begin establishing a relationship and helping ease any homesickness or separation anxiety. Assigning youngsters a "buddy" to help with orientation and allowing them to bring "transitional objects" from home also may facilitate their transition. Youngsters entering long-term residential treatment especially need reassurance of frequent contact with people at home and in the community; phone, mail, and visitation policies should be reviewed.

A key element of the admissions process in both inpatient and residential settings is the development of a written, individualized, comprehensive treatment plan. This plan identifies the various problem areas to be addressed as well as the interventions to be used. Ideally, the plan also specifies the youth's strengths, which can serve as a basis for further development and skill-building. The language and concepts of the treatment plan may be primarily psychodynamic, developmental, growth oriented, or behavioral, depending on the theoretical orientation of the program. The initial treatment plan should be written immediately after admission and be reviewed and updated regularly.

Treatment plans are ideally goal driven (Barker, 1993; Berlin & Hendren, 1991; Dalton et al., 1987), with a goal identified for each problem area and related concrete, incremental objectives and interventions specified (Schultz & Dark, 1982). Objectives are optimally stated in terms of measurable outcomes, with anticipated completion dates projected. In inpatient settings, objectives are usually short-term and focus on resolving the immediate crisis. In long-term settings, objectives may initially be short-term but should be revised over time, as the resident progresses, to reflect longer term goals.

Parents or guardians and mental health or child welfare professionals from the community working with the family should be included in treatment planning. Continuity of care is enhanced, the youth's treatment is integrated into the larger framework of ongoing work with the family, and the family is engaged in the child's treatment. Youngsters should also participate in their own treatment planning to the extent that they are capable; at a minimum, their treatment plans should be explained to them in age-appropriate language, and their feedback should be sought (Jacob & Hartshorne, 1991; Koocher, 1976; Koocher & Keith-Spiegel, 1990).

THE TREATMENT TEAM

Treatment is commonly planned and directed by an interdisciplinary treatment team (Kerlinsky, 1991). In this approach, representatives from the various health and mental health disciplines meet regularly to discuss a youngster's progress and to update treatment planning as needed. On-line staff might contribute observations as well that are gleaned from their close and daily contact with the youngster, and behavioral data and other evaluations should be reviewed. A member of the team often serves as coordinator of treatment and helps staff integrate their input and update plans as needed. Professional staff typically provide oversight, direction, and specific therapies while on-line staff implement the therapeutic milieu and daily routines and protocols.

Disciplines represented on the treatment team often include clinical psychology, clinical social work, counseling, special education, psychiatry, therapeutic recreation, and, in more medical settings, psychiatric nursing (Kaplan & Sadock, 1985; Lewis & Summerville, 1991). Referrals are made as needed to specialists in nutrition, occupational therapy, speech and hearing services, neurology, neuropsychology, pediatrics, and other relevant health and mental health fields. The psychiatrist's initial focus is the youngster's current mental status, medical and medication history, and current medical and medication needs. The psychiatrist also may help formulate the dynamics of the case in consultation with other mental health professionals on the treatment team. The clinical psychologist's role in assessment usually involves assisting in making differential diagnoses, identifying patient strengths and weaknesses relevant to treatment, and recommending psychological treatment interventions. The psychologist draws upon observation, interviews, and psychological tests that help establish a patient's cognitive as well as emotional and behavioral functioning. Psychologists also serve as group, individual, and family therapists. Clinical social workers may fulfill a variety of roles as well. Traditionally, however, their training has focused on working with children and adolescents in the context of their communities and families. They are particularly well-prepared to serve as liaisons with referral and resource agencies and to provide family services. They often coordinate both the admissions and discharge process and also serve as therapists. Special educators are trained to provide academic assessment and instruction to youngsters with learning disabilities, mental retardation, and/or significant emotional and behavioral problems that interfere with their ability to perform academically. As members of the treatment team, they advise their colleagues regarding clients' educational needs and, with the team, decide when to refer students to community schools. Teachers also serve as liaisons with staff in the clients' schools outside the hospital and residential settings to help ensure continuity and follow-up in the clients' schooling.

Treatment teams seem to function best when the administrative structure is relatively flat rather than hierarchical, that is, when supervisory and professional staff are readily accessible to on-line staff, interacting and communicating frequently (Rindfleisch, 1993). Problems can get addressed quickly, crisis intervention can be timely, and supervision and support can be immediate. Also, administrative and professional staff can be familiar firsthand with the problems and needs of the program, and on-line staff can feel more integrated into the administrative structure. The unit or program director also needs to be accessible to all staff—on-line, professional, and administrative—whether he or she directs one or several programs (Diamond, 1993). Work in a residential treatment program can be highly stressful; a supportive environment with open communication channels helps reduce that stress and enhance staff performance.

An alternative to the interdisciplinary treatment team model employs a case manager who coordinates treatment for a particular youngster from admission to discharge (Lewis & Summerville, 1991). It is the case manager's responsibility to follow the case closely, making sure that all needed services are provided and serving as patient advocate. The case manager in this context typically functions in most of the major clinical and consultative roles relevant to the case—for example, conducting individual and family therapy, consulting with other members of the treatment team and with mental health professionals in the community, arranging aftercare appointments—and leads the discussion of the case at treatment planning meetings. Typically, social work, psychology, or counseling staff serve as case managers.

AFTERCARE PLANNING

Long-term outcomes for children and adolescents are highly dependent on the quality and availability of transition and aftercare services and support (Cornsweet, 1990; Friedman & Street, 1985; Maluccio, 1993; Tuma, 1989; Wells, 1991; Whittaker et al., 1989). Consequently, well before a youngster leaves an inpatient or residential treatment facility, a comprehensive and coordinated transition plan should be developed in consultation with parents or guardians and the social service agencies or mental health professionals who will be providing aftercare. Any particularly dangerous behaviors need to be addressed specifically (e.g., continuing risk of suicide or sexual aggression). Aftercare should facilitate permanency planning for the child or adolescent (Galaway, 1991) and ideally includes strong case management and individualized services (Friedman & Street, 1985). Specifying aftercare plans helps ensure continuity of treatment because staff identify and collaborate with those likely to be involved in the youth's future. As discharge approaches, the phase-out and aftercare plans also help staff to prepare patients for their particular transitions, such as being reunited with family or moving into a new foster home. Ample transition time should be allowed as residents leave long-term treatment, especially if the resident will be moving into a new placement setting. Trial visits to home and school often help the phase-out go more smoothly. To facilitate continuity of care, some hospitals and residential centers provide aftercare services such as family support and periodic monitoring of the child's adjustment. Others rely on community resources for these and other services (Berlin & Hendren, 1991; Lewis & Summerville, 1991).

COMPONENTS OF INPATIENT AND RESIDENTIAL TREATMENT

Length of patient stay varies across the various types of inpatient settings, and some hospitals provide long-term treatment. However, most inpatient settings accommodate emergency admissions and provide primarily acute and short-term to intermediate-length care (Dalton et al., 1987; Gadpaille, 1985; Jemerin & Phillips, 1988; Woolston, 1991). Such programs emphasize crisis intervention, rapid assessment, stabilization, and short-term treatment toward short-term goals. In contrast, residential treatment usually focuses more holistically on residents' longer term growth and development.

Residential treatment centers vary greatly in the services they provide, but a therapeutic milieu is typically considered the central element of treatment (Kaplan & Sadock, 1985; Woolston, 1991). Other services often include medication monitoring, mental health services, schooling, family support, and mental health consultation. Some centers expand mental health services into a comprehensive program composed of therapy, psychoeducational groups, and therapeutic recreation. Often, programs with a strong family commitment also provide parent training, family therapy, and other family services.

Psychiatric and Medication Monitoring

In medical settings, inpatients are monitored daily for psychotropic medication needs, and medications are frequently prescribed by patients' psychiatrists to target chronic and acute difficulties. Medications prescribed include neuroleptics (antipsychotic medication), psychostimulants (e.g., targeting attention deficits), anxiolytic medications (e.g., targeting sleep disorders and anxiety), and antidepressants (Handen, 1995; Kaplan & Sadock, 1985; Moss, 1994; Tuma, 1989; Wiener, 1985). Medical, nursing, and mental health staff monitor patients for benefits and for side effects such as tardive dyskinesia when phenothiazines are prescribed. Many children and adolescents in residential treatment also take some form of psychotropic medication. The medications are monitored and prescribed by a psychiatrist, ideally a child/adolescent psychiatrist, who consults with or serves on the treatment team. The psychiatrist also provides staff direction as needed in monitoring for the benefits and side effects of the medications prescribed (Lewis & Summerville, 1991).

Diagnostic and Evaluation Services

Psychiatrists and clinical psychologists observe and conduct clinical interviews and formal mental status examinations with inpatients. Formal psychological testing is often conducted as well (e.g., to assist with making differential diagnoses and establishing a patient's cognitive strengths and weaknesses). Psychoeducational evaluations, by psychology and/or education staff, help further identify any academic deficits or learning disabilities. Interviews and testing conducted with family members help identify family systems liabilities and strengths (Kaplan & Sadock, 1985).

In residential treatment settings, residents' mental status also should be evaluated regularly by mental health professionals. Comprehensive psychiatric and psychological evaluations also might be needed, but much evaluation is often completed prior to a resident's admission and need not be duplicated needlessly (Kaplan & Sadock, 1985). As the resident's stay progresses, however, certain evaluations must be updated regularly (e.g., to determine whether certain special education services continue to be needed). New problems may be identified that require additional formal evaluation as well (Lewis & Summerville, 1991).

Mental Health and Psychoeducational Services

Specific mental health and psychoeducational services provided to children and adolescents include individual, group, and family therapy; crisis intervention; psychoeducational activities; occupational, recreational, and art therapies; and sometimes joint therapy, when two children are seen together in therapy (Gwynn, Meyer, & Schaefer, 1993; Kaplan & Sadock, 1985; Lewis & Summerville, 1991; Moss, 1994; Ney & Mulvihill, 1985; Tuma, 1989). Individual therapy can vary greatly in form and content, depending on the needs of the particular child and orientation of the therapist, but generally follows a psychodynamic, behavioral, or cognitive model. Some younger, traumatized children may benefit from unstructured play therapy; older children may be capable of participating in verbal, insight-oriented psychotherapy. Cognitive-behavioral therapies have been shown to be effective with a wide range of presenting problems, including impulsivity (Kendall & Finch, 1978). Joint therapy is employed less frequently but is an option when two children are compatible developmentally and seem capable of learning from each other under the therapist's direction (Gwynn et al., 1993).

Group therapy often addresses dynamics of behavior and the processing of feelings. In such groups, children and adolescents express their concerns, serve as models for each other, provide each other support, and develop age-appropriate insight into their problems (McFadden, 1992; Tuma, 1989). Group therapy also includes specialized groups, such as those exploring grief issues, substance abuse, or sexual abuse (Doyle & Bauer, 1989; Stearns, 1991; Zahn, 1991). Depending on the theoretical orientation of the therapists and needs of the children, other sorts of group therapy may be offered.

Psychoeducational services include skill-building groups and patient education through bibliotherapy (Pardeck, 1992), instruction, discussion, videotapes, therapeutic games and other activities, modeling, and feedback. Patients learn about their symptomatic behavior, for example, and the benefits and side effects of their medications—in age-appropriate terms, of course. Other topics pertinent to most child and adolescent groups include good health habits, coping with family dysfunction, alcohol and other drug use and abuse, and sex education. The latter two topics are especially important for preadolescent and adolescent residents (Crenshaw, 1993; Kaplan & Sadock, 1985). Social skills training is important for both children and adolescents in residential treatment because they usually have poorly developed social skills and because social competence is positively correlated with long-term prognosis (Cox & Schopler, 1991). In social skills groups, youngsters may learn how to listen actively, communicate more effectively, "read" facial expressions and body language, identify others' perspectives, make friends, join groups, interact cooperatively, be assertive rather than aggressive, and generally develop prosocial interpersonal skills. Mental health services may also include therapeutic recreation, which helps youngsters learn cooperative team play, coordination and athletic skills, and sportsmanship in a therapeutic context. Art, dance, occupational, and other therapies also may be included, depending on a program's resources and orientation (Johnson, 1990).

Most therapeutic and skill-building activities are selected for theoretical reasons (e.g., teaching self-control techniques to impulsive children) (Schneider & Robin, 1976). However, empirical research is beginning to demonstrate the relative effectiveness of selected treatment approaches with residential clients. Small and Schinke (1983), for example, have demonstrated with latency-age boys in residential treatment that a program teaching social competence (by combining interpersonal, cognitive, problem-solving training with interpersonal communications skill training) was more effective in improving the boys' ability to generate alternative solutions to problems than either discussion groups or interpersonal, cognitive, problem-solving training alone. Boys receiving the social competence training also were rated by classroom teachers on measures of aggressive and nonaggressive acting-out as behaving more appropriately than their peers.

Teaching youngsters to inhibit aggression and develop more constructive expressions of anger is especially important in long-term treatment settings, where many residents have chronic problems with aggressive, destructive acting-out. Two main behavioral approaches used are contingency management and cognitive-behavioral training, including instruction, modeling, and feedback (Elder, Edelstein, & Narick, 1979). Aggression Replacement Training (ART) (Goldstein & Glick, 1994) and its forerunner, Structured Learning Therapy (SLT) (Goldstein, Sherman, Gershaw, Sprafkin, & Glick, 1978), have been implemented effectively in both community and residential treatment settings. Based on a behavior deficiency model of aggression, which posits that aggressive youth typically lack alternative prosocial skills, ART is a psychoeducational, multimodal intervention that combines "skillstreaming" (teaching prosocial behaviors systematically), anger control training based on Feindler, Marriott, and Iwata's (1984, in Goldstein & Glick, 1994) original model, and moral education. Both ART and SLT employ modeling, role playing, performance feedback and social reinforcement, and transfer training strategies (Goldstein & Glick, 1994; Goldstein et al., 1978). The anger control component of ART focuses on teaching self-control of anger. Moral education attempts to raise youngsters' sense of fairness, justice, and recognition of the needs and rights of others (Goldstein & Glick, 1994). Specific prosocial skills components taught range from "beginning social skills" to "planning skills." The "skill alternatives to aggression" component includes such specific skills as "avoiding trouble with others" and "keeping out of fights" (Goldstein et al., 1978).

Elder et al. (1979) have also reported success in modifying the aggressive behavior of hospitalized adolescents with a similar social skills training program, and Schneider (1991) has demonstrated the usefulness of both skill-building and relaxation/desensitization interventions targeting aggression in children in residential treatment. Recently, LeCroy (1988) has demonstrated in a long-term residential treatment setting the relative efficacy of "anger management" training (teaching socially competent alternatives to aggression as a means of coping with anger) over "anger expression" (based on an often-cited but empirically questionable catharsis model of decreasing aggressiveness) in reducing adolescent females' choices of aggressive alternatives in solving problems.

Staff providing mental health and psychoeducational services should have not only the education, credentials, and supervision necessary for competency in their particular position, but they also should have special expertise in working with issues common among children and adolescents in their treatment program. In residential treatment settings, these issues often include the sequelae of physical, sexual, and emotional abuse; loss, separation, rejection, and abandonment concerns; interpersonal trust and vulnerability issues that manifest in many ways (e.g., in adapting to foster care); and, for many children no longer in the custody of their parents, idealizations of family and hopes for reunion (Doyle & Bauer, 1989; McFadden, 1992; Swanson & Schaefer, 1993).

Family Services

Therapists have long recognized that children's adjustment depends greatly on the adequacy of parenting and family relationships, and

therapists are increasingly recognizing that a child's symptomatic behavior typically signals dysfunction in the family system rather than
simply individual psychopathology (Barker, 1993). Research also shows
that family involvement in a child's residential treatment is positively
correlated with the child's improvement during and after treatment
(Prentice-Dunn et al., 1981; Whittaker et al., 1989; Whittaker & Pecora,
1984). Consequently, inpatient and residential treatment programs often
provide youngsters' families an array of services including parent
training (Dalton et al., 1987; Ney & Mulvihill, 1985) and family therapy
(Ravenscroft, 1991). Parents may participate in impromptu conferences
with staff as well as scheduled discussions of treatment and academic
progress and planning. Other family services include support groups,
visits on- and off-campus, and education (e.g., about a child's behavioral and emotional difficulties and any medications the child takes)
(Krona, 1980; Lewis & Summerville, 1991; Magnus, 1974). Family
support is important during any crises that develop and also in such
matters as helping family members deal with their child's absence from
home and generally supporting the family's strengths, coping skills, and
relationships.

When a child is not returning to his or her family to live, family issues
should still be addressed. This may be accomplished to some degree in
individual therapy, where issues of loss, abandonment, grief, and anger
may be explored. The parents also may be helped to facilitate the child's
acceptance of placement outside the home of origin and to resolve other
family issues (Carlo, 1985; Kaplan & Sadock, 1985). Foster family
members may also participate (e.g., to help children understand any
"failed" placements they have experienced and to cope with changes in
placement) (Carlo, 1985).

Mental Health Consultation

Whenever children or adolescents come to a residential treatment
setting, they are almost invariably already involved in the "system of
care" and thus in a network of people interested in the child's welfare,
many of whom will continue to be involved with them during and after
their residence. Once proper consents to obtain and release information
are signed by parents or other guardians, and depending on the particulars of the case, residential program staff may need to confer with health
and mental health professionals, child welfare personnel, educators,
attorneys, guardians ad-litem, judges, juvenile court staff, and/or pro-

bation officers. Regular and open communication facilitates treatment planning and continuity of care after discharge. Maintaining a youngster's other ties to the community is also important (Wilson & Lyman, 1983), especially to help facilitate generalization of treatment effects beyond the treatment setting. Helpful strategies include returning the youngster to a community school as soon as feasible and scheduling regular visits home or to visiting resources.

Special Education

Special education needs are highly correlated with severe psychological problems in children and adolescents. Intellectual limitations, specific learning disabilities, and underachievement occur frequently along with behavioral and emotional difficulties (Kaplan & Sadock, 1985; Lewis & Summerville, 1991; Woolston, Rosenthal, & Riddle, 1989, in Woolston, 1991). Consequently, many residential treatment programs provide their own in-house special education programs (Kaplan & Sadock, 1985; Lewis & Summerville, 1991). In these, residents typically learn to attend, cooperate, and perform academically in small, structured classrooms with a low child-to-staff ratio. Trained to provide services for emotionally disturbed and/or learning disabled children, teachers may be assisted by classroom aides who provide additional individual assistance to students. In consultation with other members of the treatment team, the classroom teacher should design a classroom environment and behavior management strategies to motivate students to behave and perform well academically.

Residential Programming

Along with special education services, residential (i.e., home setting) programming comprises the core of treatment in a residential treatment center (Kaplan & Sadock, 1985; Lewis & Summerville, 1991). In the home and school settings, residents experience the therapeutic milieu most intensely because they interact with classroom and residential staff in the course of their daily lives. The residential setting is usually a small group home living arrangement with a low resident-to-staff ratio. In the home, residents learn to live together with peers and adults, sharing meals, chores, and leisure time. Residents learn coping and problem-solving skills and, it is hoped, build relationships with peers and staff. They should also learn such basic living skills as maintaining personal hygiene, their personal items, and their living space. Because residents are often deficient in adaptive skills, social skills, and self-control, all of these potentially are the focus of therapeutic interactions. As residents progress, staff should encourage greater independence but continue to provide developmentally appropriate assistance as needed. Like other treatment components, the residential program should be quite structured so that youngsters follow a predictable routine. The programming should be flexible, however, so that special occasions and individual needs can be accommodated. Time should also be allowed for structured play and free time. Play is a developmentally important activity of childhood, as is age-appropriate recreation in adolescence. In play, youngsters try out new roles, develop new physical and interpersonal skills, and develop self-esteem. Residents need opportunities for normal as well as therapeutic play (McFadden, 1992; Mercer, 1982).

Residential staffing may follow either a houseparent or rotating staff model. In the former, staff live with the residents around the clock, with different sets of houseparents alternating periodically to allow each other time off. Rotating staff work in shifts: one shift works 8 to 12 hours, then the next shift begins. Rotating staff are typically employed in settings where it is necessary that staff be awake and supervising residents at all times, rather than sleeping through the night. With conduct-disordered children and adolescents, the latter model is usually warranted (Zimmerman, 1994).

Hiring standards for staff vary by center, but in most, an initial orientation period and supervised on-the-job training comprise the core of job-relevant training. Key job requirements are that the person exhibit the personal maturity, good judgment, self-control, stress tolerance, interpersonal skills, and ability to develop emotional connections with children and adolescents necessary to work daily with difficult clients. Background checks and references are needed to help screen out job applicants whose histories suggest they would not be safe or effective working with children.

SUMMARY

Inpatient settings are usually considered the most intensive, restrictive, and secure psychiatric treatment settings. Children and adolescents are typically admitted in crisis and present with dangerous or seriously deteriorated behavior. Diagnostically, young inpatients often exhibit disruptive behavior disorders, mood disorders, psychoses, organic brain syndromes, or pervasive developmental disorders. Treatment is usually short-term and oriented toward crisis intervention and stabilization.

Children and adolescents admitted to residential treatment programs usually exhibit chronic, multiple problem behaviors that may be dangerous or potentially dangerous. These youngsters typically have been involved with social service, mental health, juvenile justice, and/or special education services prior to their admission to residential treatment but have not responded adequately to previous interventions. They often come from dysfunctional, unstable families, and many are no longer in their parents' homes or custody. Relative to their siblings and peers, youngsters entering residential treatment often demonstrate significant skills deficits, such as in academic and social competency. Common psychiatric diagnoses include disruptive behavior disorders, mood disorders, and posttraumatic stress disorders.

In both inpatient and residential treatment settings, treatment planning should be individualized, multidisciplinary, and goal driven, and it should allow for participation by the youngsters. Goals are more immediate in inpatient treatment and longer term and more holistic in residential settings. Long-term prognosis depends heavily upon family involvement in treatment and upon the adequacy of resources and support provided after youngsters are discharged. Thus, it is critical to provide for family support, parent training, family therapy, and aftercare services.

Other services provided in inpatient and residential programs include psychiatric monitoring, medication monitoring, diagnostic and evaluation services, mental health consultation, individual and group psychotherapy, psychoeducational programming, special education, and provision of a therapeutic milieu. Staff providing services need to have special expertise in working with issues common to their patient population. In residential treatment, for example, treatment issues often include the sequelae of physical, sexual, and emotional abuse; loss, separation, rejection, and abandonment concerns; interpersonal trust and vulnerability issues; and significant deficits in academic, coping, and social skills. Most therapeutic activities are selected for theoretical reasons, but empirical research is beginning to demonstrate the relative effectiveness of selected treatment approaches. For example, certain social skills and aggression-reduction programs have been shown to be effective with residential clients.

NOTES

1. Critics question claims that most hospitalized children and adolescents are dangerous either to self or others. Weithorn (1988), for example, attributed "skyrocketing" adolescent admission rates to private inpatient programs in the early 1980s to sociopolitical and economic factors rather than increased psychopathology among young people. She views most hospitalized youth as "troublesome" rather than mentally ill and advocates the development of better community-based treatment programs for these youth and their families. Mental health professionals also have voiced concern about reducing inappropriate hospital admissions (e.g., see Steinberg, Galhenage, & Robinson, 1981), and advocates of community-based treatment have developed out-of-hospital interventions even for youngsters exhibiting dangerous behavior such as suicidal ideation and intention (Bereika & Mikkelsen, 1992).

2. Tuma (1989) reports that approximately 15% of residential treatment facilities provide long-term treatment for severely disturbed children not expected to develop normally (e.g., autistic or severely retarded children).

3

THE THERAPEUTIC MILIEU: DAILY TREATMENT AND CRISIS INTERVENTION

Whether the setting is inpatient or residential, the program's therapeutic milieu, or overall atmosphere, is an important feature of treatment (Dalton, Bolding, Woods, & Daruna, 1987; Irwin, 1987). This is especially true for children and adolescents in residential treatment. Their emotional and behavioral difficulties often appear caused or exacerbated by chronically inconsistent, unstable, or even chaotic relationships and home environments, as discussed in the previous chapter. The stability of a therapeutic environment is critical, so that the milieu may continually shape and inform a child's or adolescent's experiences. It provides adaptive experiences that the client presumably has missed in the course of growing up, and it also provides corrective experiences to offset some of the more damaging experiences the resident has had. Ideally, residents will learn not to contribute unwittingly to their own behavior problems and victimization. In particular, the milieu initially provides external structure and control for the severely disturbed child or adolescent who lacks adequate self-control. This external control should be relaxed as the youngster becomes more proficient at self-regulation.

ELEMENTS OF THE THERAPEUTIC MILIEU

Although interpreted in various ways depending on a clinician's theoretical perspective, the following are some of the more critical features of a therapeutic milieu recognized by mental health professionals (e.g., Bleiberg, 1989; Colyar, 1991; Lambert, 1977; Schaefer & Swanson, 1993; Thomas, 1982; Wilson & Lyman, 1983).

Safety and Health

The single most important feature of the therapeutic milieu is its guarantee of physical and psychological safety. Physical safety is promoted through the design and maintenance of a safe physical environment, provision of adequate nutrition and activities fostering healthy growth, provision of appropriate medical services, careful screening and supervision of employees, provision of written policy to guide staff interventions, training of staff to use only safe intervention methods, monitoring of interventions, a child-to-staff ratio that allows for adequate supervision of residents, and observation of standard universal safety precaution procedures (Gil, 1982; Lewis & Summerville, 1991; McGrath, 1991; Murray & Sefchik, 1992; Nevin, 1993; Rindfleisch, 1993; Thomas, 1982). Psychological safety is fostered by treating children and adolescents in caring, fair, humane, respectful, and predictable ways (Dahms, 1978). It is especially important for staff to build trust with clients who have difficulty developing attachments because of prior abuse, neglect, disrupted family relationships, or other trauma (Doyle & Bauer, 1989; Small, Kennedy, & Bender, 1991) and to recognize multicultural differences that are important to clients (Vargas & Berlin, 1991). Staff need to be selected, trained, supported, and supervised to be therapeutic and collaborative and, especially, to avoid noxious or abusive attitudes and behaviors (Gil, 1982; Lewis & Summerville, 1991; Rindfleisch, 1993; Robin, 1982; Shealy, 1995).

Protection of Children's and Adolescents' Rights

All of children's and adolescents' legal, ethical, and humanitarian rights must be respected at all times, at all levels, and within all interactions relevant to the client. These rights should be stated in program policy manuals, discussed in staff training and supervision, and communicated to the clients, their families, and others involved in the care and monitoring of the child's or adolescent's well-being. Ideally, a statement of clients' rights is posted conspicuously for easy consultation by clients, their visitors, and staff (Thomas, 1982). Clinicians may need to be proactive in advocating for children's rights and treatment needs (Small & Otto, 1991; Thies, 1976). Specific rights include those guaranteeing the youth protection (e.g., from physical harm and environmental dangers), sustenance (including nutritional food and a stable relationship with a parent or other caretaker), treatment (including medical, dental, and mental health services), and services fostering developmental progress both academically and socially. Within hospitals and residential treatment settings, which impose at least some impediments to a resident's ordinary freedoms, additional rights are relevant: freedom from undue invasion of privacy, right of access to family and friends, and right to respect for one's cultural and religious values (Kramer, 1994; Thomas, 1982).

Confidentiality, an especially important right protected by legal and ethical standards, requires that the privacy of clients and their families be respected and that the confidentiality of patient information be preserved at all times unless legal, informed consent to release specified information to specified parties for specified reasons is given by the child's or adolescent's legal guardian (Koocher & Keith-Spiegel, 1990). In practical terms, this means that staff do not exchange information about a case with third parties, either verbally or by sharing written documents, unless and until the necessary consent has been obtained. Staff must be especially careful when taking phone calls for or inquiring about particular individuals to be sure that the client's involvement in treatment is not unwittingly verified for a person who does not have legal access to that information.

In contrast to the general rule of preserving confidentiality, there are a few instances in which otherwise confidential information must be shared with third parties. All states have abuse reporting laws, for example, and most specify mental health professionals among those required to report suspected abuse. Also, there could be instances in which therapists have a "duty-to-protect" a third party deemed at risk of harm (Koocher & Keith-Spiegel, 1990).

Matters related to confidentiality are more complicated when addressed with respect to communication inside the inpatient or residential setting and with youngsters' families. As Gadpaille (1985) has observed, the legal status of young patients, especially adolescents, is ambiguous, and at times, clinicians must make difficult judgment calls regarding whether and how to disclose information shared by a young client. The general guideline is that when family or staff have a legitimate need to know (e.g., to protect the child's well-being), information may be shared. Ethical and clinical principles should guide the selection of material to be shared and the manner in which the information is shared, and these guidelines need to be addressed in program policies. Youngsters, especially adolescents, need to be apprised early on in therapy of the limits of confidentiality and, circumstances permitting, should be offered the opportunity to discuss in advance any anticipated disclosures. Parents, too, need to be prepared regarding the nature and limits of confidentiality (Gadpaille, 1985; Jacob & Hartshorne, 1991; Koocher, 1976; Koocher & Keith-Spiegel, 1990). All staff should be careful not to discuss a youngster with other youngsters, and they need to be sure not to discuss a youngster among themselves within earshot of the youth or his or her peers (Lambert, 1977). On-line, nonprofessional staff may not selectively withhold information confided by a youngster from professional staff.

Positive, Supportive Approach

Overall, the treatment environment should be positive, nurturing, and upbeat rather than punitive or repressive in tone. Youngsters' dependency needs should be met, and birthdays, holidays, and other special occasions should be celebrated (Cormack, 1993b). Treatment should build on patients' strengths and employ positive intervention strategies such as the systematic use of positive reinforcement and the promotion of positive staff-child relationships (Krumboltz & Krumboltz, 1972; Swanson & Richard, 1993). Staff should serve as positive role models for identification. Some programs, especially psychodynamically oriented ones, carefully foster staff-resident relationships as the critical (Lyth, 1985) therapeutic element in residential treatment (Bleiberg, 1989; Maier, 1975; Shealy, 1995; Thomas, 1989).

A positive approach is important for practical, clinical, and humane reasons. Positive reinforcement as a behavior modification technique, for example, is effective (Murray & Sefchik, 1992), and it is more easily used safely and correctly than is punishment or other aversive teaching strategies (Krumboltz & Krumboltz, 1972). Positive relationships with adults in caretaking and authority positions allow youngsters to meet their dependency needs age-appropriately and provide corrective emotional experiences for those who do not trust or identify with adults. Positive relationships with staff also enhance the staff's authority with youngsters and promote the youngster's development of internal control (Bleiberg, 1989; Dahms, 1978; Miller, 1986). Staff should be careful to avoid becoming engaged in negative interactions with youth that can spiral into coercive cycles (Goren, Abraham, & Doyle, in press; Goren, Singh, & Best, 1993; Natta, Holmbeck, Kupst, Pines, & Schulman, 1990).

Prior to their admission to residential treatment, many residents have experienced repeated failures, rejections, and even abuse and neglect.

They are often more familiar with negative than with positive forms of attention, and many have adopted the uncontrolled and violent behaviors of models within their homes or communities, often being intrinsically or extrinsically reinforced for acting-out. Others have organically based impulse control problems. Staff can expect residents initially to exhibit considerable maladaptive behavior and to need firm limits, much support, and external motivators to help them begin behaving more adaptively. External motivators may include special privileges or treats used as rewards. Some programs employ token economies or systems of "levels" of privileges in which residents earn increasingly attractive privileges as they behave more adaptively (Moss, 1994). Over time, as relationships with staff become meaningful, social reinforcers such as staff interest, praise, and approval become powerful motivators as well. Lacking skills and tolerating frustration poorly, youngsters new to treatment typically require short reinforcement intervals and frequent reminders of the rewards and activities they may enjoy if they behave adaptively. Even small increments of improved behavior need to be recognized. As youngsters become better at delaying gratification and more skilled in executing more complex behavior, longer term goals should be introduced.

Obviously, staff will have unpleasant interactions with their clients at times, such as when imposing a resisted limit or physically restraining a violent child. However, these can be ultimately positive experiences for the child or adolescent if handled properly and followed up constructively. Youngsters can learn that staff have positive expectations for them, will not take their acting-out as a personal affront, will not engage (Beker & Feuerstein, 1991) in power struggles, and will not retaliate against those who act out (Bleiberg, 1989; McGrath, 1991).

Normalization

The residential treatment environment, although not a natural or normal environment for the patient, should be designed to provide as many normal experiences as possible. This is especially important for children and adolescents in long-term treatment to prevent them becoming institutionalized (e.g., too dependent on staff direction, talking in jargon, losing spontaneity) and to promote the generalization of their learning when they move back into a more normal environment (Gadpaille, 1985). Normalization can be accomplished in many ways. Most conspicuously, the physical environment, routines, and rules can approximate those of normal homes as much as possible. For example, residents could decorate their rooms with personal items or eat homestyle together with peers and staff at small tables. Clients' behavior, when appropriate, needs to be normalized as well. That is, staff need to help children differentiate between normal and unhealthy behavior (e.g., between normal sexual curiosity and pathological sexual acting-out) (Johnson & Aoki, 1993). Children and adolescents in long-term treatment also need to have experiences outside the treatment setting and relationships with people outside the treatment facility. Such experiences can include going to public school, having regular home visits with family or friends, and spending time regularly with a mentor or friend from the community (Gwynn, Meyer, & Schaefer, 1993).

Individualization and Flexibility

In both inpatient and residential treatment settings, the formal treatment plans for clients should be appropriately individualized. That is, treatment should be adapted to accommodate the needs of the particular client. Some standard interventions might not be appropriate for a particular child or adolescent because of his or her history or cultural background (Vargas & Berlin, 1991), and clients sometimes exhibit problems not addressed adequately, if at all, in the usual program. In the former case, alternative interventions should be developed. In the latter, either an individualized behavior management plan or a referral for supplementary treatment outside the residential setting is needed.

It is especially important for the therapeutic milieu and treatment protocols in residential treatment centers to be flexible enough to accommodate individual interests, strengths, and treatment needs of the children or adolescents in residence. Such individualized programming helps prevent institutionalization and promotes the client's overall development. Residents' interests and strengths may be reinforced by staff members spending extra time with a youngster with whom they share a common interest, such as in writing, arts and crafts, or sports. When they are able behaviorally to participate, children and adolescents also may be referred to special interest groups, classes, or social and recreational groups that meet in the community.

It is important for treatment programming to be flexible in other ways besides accommodating individual patients' needs. As groups present with more severe conduct problems, for example, structure and supervision for all clients might need to be tightened (Colyar, 1991). As admissions trends vary, topics for group discussion might need to change to remain developmentally appropriate and focused on relevant issues.

Developmental Appropriateness

Although there is considerable similarity between the difficulties of younger children and adolescents in residential treatment (Wurtele, Wilson, & Prentice-Dunn, 1983), work with adolescents should differ from that with children in a number of significant ways (Gadpaille, 1985; Kaplan & Sadock, 1985; Lambert, 1977; Miller & Burt, 1982). Therapy and discussions should address the specific developmental concerns of teenagers (e.g., regarding sexuality, peer acceptance, and increasing autonomy) as well as the clinical problems likely to first manifest in adolescence (such as substance abuse and eating disorders). Adolescents also often require especially firm limits regarding aggressive and sexual acting-out. Peer influence should be recognized and fostered as a constructive force for behavior change (Gwynn et al., 1993), and therapeutic modalities can be selected to appeal to adolescent interests in risk-taking and excitement by including, for example, outdoor, adventure-based activities (Beker & Feuerstein, 1991). In preparation for young adulthood, older adolescents often benefit from career counseling, vocationally oriented education, and the acquisition of independent living skills such as those involved in job hunting and managing an apartment.

Structure

Structure refers to the boundaries and organization that all youngsters need for healthy functioning and development. These are particularly important in acute inpatient care because almost all the children or adolescents admitted to such programs are in crisis, and external structure can help them maintain control. Structure is also important for children and adolescents in residential treatment (Romig, 1978, in Barker, 1982). Because of their behavioral and emotional deficits, these youngsters require much more structure than do most children.

The most important forms of structure are rules, behavioral limits, and daily routines. Rules should be few in number and stated clearly. Behavioral limits also need to be stated clearly, reasonable for the age and skill level of the client population, and enforceable. Routines need to allow time for school, therapeutic activities, exercise and play, meals and snacks, health and hygiene, and rest. In the residential setting, personal time, group chores, outings, and other community activities need to be included in the schedule as well. Ideally, schedules are posted and provided individually to youngsters who understand the concept of time (Johnson, 1995).

Consistency and Predictability

Along with structure, consistency and predictability provide children and adolescents with a sense of order and a known environment in which to explore new learning experiences. Consistency and predictability are created in part by programming so that clients know when to expect, say, meals or playtime. More important, however, is the consistency and predictability of staff response to children and adolescents, within and across program areas. Staff must be well-trained, must communicate effectively, and must work cooperatively as a team so that they know how to handle various situations and can support each other in doing so, especially during crises or when residents become manipulative and test limits (Lambert, 1977). Daily shift-change reporting and weekly meetings help facilitate staff communication and cohesion (Johnson, 1995). Consistency should not deteriorate into rigidity or overspecification of behavior so that youngsters are pressured to conform to a monotonously routine environment. Residents need some spontaneity and variation in experiences to develop maximally and avoid becoming institutionalized (Beker & Feuerstein, 1990, 1991; Ney & Mulvihill, 1985).

Family Orientation

In the past, residential treatment often was based on a philosophy advocating isolation of children and adolescents from the often dysfunctional environments from which they came, including isolation from their families (Carlo, 1985). Contemporary views are less judgmental and recognize that a child's family of origin, and the larger environment within which the child functions, need to be central concerns during treatment (Barker, 1982, 1993; Carlo, 1985; Cates, 1991; Kaplan & Sadock, 1985; Maluccio, 1993). Family involvement in a child's residential treatment is a predictor of the child's progress while in residence and following discharge (Carlo, 1985; Prentice-Dunn et al., 1981).

For those children and adolescents who will return to live with their families after discharge, it is critical that policies, procedures, and the treatment milieu support the family's active involvement in their child's treatment (e.g., Carlo, 1985; Durrant, 1993; Krona, 1980; Magnus, 1974; Ney & Mulvihill, 1985). Parents need to participate in the decision to refer the child for treatment, assist in the admissions and treatment planning process, participate in regular reviews of their child's progress, participate in the therapeutic milieu, and be involved in planning for the child's discharge and aftercare needs. Frequent family contact by mail, phone, and visits is critical for residents to help preserve and strengthen the emotional bonds within the family.

Families usually need to be engaged in therapy, especially to help create a family focus for change rather than unduly emphasizing the psychopathology of the child who has been designated the patient (Ravenscroft, 1991; Tuma, 1989). The goal is to help the whole family system change. The parents often need help with parenting and behavior management skills as well as dealing with their own feelings of guilt, inadequacy, and being overwhelmed.

Working with these families can be a challenge. Besides geographic and economic barriers often present, sociocultural differences and family dynamics are often difficult to navigate (Carlo, 1985; Hagen, 1993). If parents are available and able to participate in treatment, their attitudes may vary from cooperation to ambivalence about their child's absence from home to resentment at their perceived loss of autonomy to envy of the nurturing their child receives in treatment. Fundamental affective relationships may be difficult to alter. Nevertheless, families often benefit from support and functional changes such as reducing stress, improving communication, and elaborating their social support network (Carlo, 1985; Goldberg, 1991; Romig, 1978, in Barker, 1982; Small et al., 1991; Wells & Whittington, 1993). Parents may also learn more about child development and effective child management techniques (Ney & Mulvihill, 1985; Ravenscroft, 1991; Tuma, 1989).

Many children and adolescents in residential treatment will not be able to return to live with their families after discharge. In some cases, custody has been removed from the parents, and the children will be placed into foster care or a group home. For these children and adolescents, it is nevertheless usually in their best interest to help preserve their family ties—or at least to help youngsters clarify whether they desire ongoing contact and in what form (Keith-Lucas, 1987). As the attachment literature indicates (Shealy, 1995), relationships with primary caretakers typically remain primary for children. Their sense of identity and self-worth are often damaged if these relationships are not maintained. Children may be helped to understand that their parent or parents care about them and want to be involved in their lives (assuming that is the case), even if the parents are unable to take care of them (Kaplan & Sadock, 1985). Parents may be involved in this process (Carlo, 1985). When the family chooses not to participate in their child's life, staff need to provide support and assistance as the child comes to accept this reality.

Therapeutic Communication and Behavior Management

Most standards of care require that staff use the least intrusive methods that will successfully address a problem behavior (Jones & Downing, 1991). Some inappropriate behaviors can be handled most effectively, for example, with selective ignoring. Behaviors that can be tolerated while the positive reinforcement of staff attention is withheld (e.g., unpleasant but largely innocuous behavior such as grumbling or muttering quietly about tasks, or nondisruptive, attention-seeking behavior such as silly or provocative remarks) often extinguish without direct staff intervention. Such behaviors are especially likely to diminish if other, appropriate behaviors, including those incompatible with the ignored behavior, are simultaneously reinforced (Johnson, 1995; Krumboltz & Krumboltz, 1972; Swanson & Richard, 1993).

Some inappropriate behaviors cannot be ignored, however, because the behaviors are significantly disruptive or potentially dangerous. To manage such behaviors, staff should implement strategies that will ultimately redirect residents to constructive behavior, a process that has been described as involving three phases: (a) stopping the inappropriate behavior as soon as possible, (b) mediation, and (c) reinvolving the child or adolescent in the milieu (Kuster, Rowland, Schaeffner, & Kupfersmid, 1988). Staff should move from the least intrusive mediation methods, such as verbal redirection, verbal deescalation, or problem solving, to more intrusive methods, such as imposing a time-out, only when the youngster fails to respond constructively early in the sequence of interventions.

Early, preventive interventions can be as simple as nonverbal communication through eye contact, facial expression, and physical proximity of staff (Kuster et al., 1988). Besides these behaviorally oriented methods, other noncoercive methods such as reframing and paradoxical techniques may be used (Durrant, 1993; Schultz, 1991). In "prescribing the symptom," for example, a client's maladaptive behavior might be interpreted as a creative adaptation whose performance is encouraged until, it is hoped, the client voluntarily relinquishes the behavior (Schultz, 1991). This strategy is similar to the behavioral intervention of satiation (Krumboltz & Krumboltz, 1972).

Mediating youngsters' learning experiences has been described as "interaction in which another human, usually the adult caregiver, interprets the world to the child" (Feuerstein & Hoffman, 1982, in Beker & Feuerstein, 1991, p. 25). To be effective in mediating with residents, the staff's messages must be therapeutic—accurately reflecting the youngster's experience, for example, or helping the youngster understand the meaning or consequences of his or her misbehavior (Schultz, 1991). Staff also need to be cognizant of how they convey these messages, in wording and nonverbal and paraverbal messages. Voice tone needs to be matter of fact and low-keyed, and stance and posture should be nonthreatening. Residents' personal space needs to be respected, along with their need to save face. Messages should be clear and simple. Throughout an intervention, staff need to work cooperatively (e.g., in providing support or respite for each other) and must resist becoming engaged in power struggles with residents or being inconsistent among themselves (Kuster et al., 1988; Lambert, 1977).

Different terms—time-out, isolation, exclusion, seclusion—are used in the literature to refer to the interruption of a resident's inappropriate behavior by removing him or her from ongoing group activities. Here, time-out is defined functionally as any form of interrupting a youngster's behavior by removing the child from positive reinforcement for a brief period—short of seclusion—until he or she becomes calm and able to participate in the ongoing activity (Swanson & Richard, 1993). Seclusion, discussed below, is defined as isolating a resident in a locked room as a crisis intervention strategy.

Time-out may be nonexclusionary, such as when a child is directed to sit apart from the group but in the same vicinity until he or she has been quiet for a few minutes—or when the child elects voluntarily to do so. Exclusionary time-outs include sending residents to their rooms, specially designed time-out rooms, or other secluded areas to be isolated from the group and most other stimulation until they are able to calm down and rejoin the group. Time-out occasionally can be used with groups, for example, when tensions among the whole group run high, and residents are becoming disruptive and escalating toward increasingly provocative and uncontrolled behavior. At these times, all residents can be instructed to take a break to calm down (Kuster et al., 1988).

In a study of time-outs given individual children in an inpatient psychiatric setting, time-outs were most often imposed for noncompliance, tantrums and loss of self-control, physical aggression, wandering, rule violation, and stealing (Jones & Downing, 1991). Ideally, time-out is employed only with escalating disruptive or aggressive behavior, that is, a behavioral sequence that must be interrupted. Other interventions or sanctions may be used to modify more discrete behaviors.

Isolation of children and adolescents from others and ongoing activities can be used for behavior management in ways other than as a time-out. Room restriction for some predetermined time, for example, may be used as a punishment for inappropriate behavior. Such practices do not function as time-out if the purpose is primarily to have residents experience an aversive consequence for inappropriate behavior. Although time-out is considered a form of punishment (response cost) that can discourage preceding inappropriate behavior, it functions primarily to interrupt a resident's inappropriate behavior and allow him or her to regain self-control and make better behavioral choices (Endres & Goke, 1973). Time-outs should be brief and terminate when a resident is no longer disruptive or escalating toward more extreme behavior. Other forms of punishment for inappropriate behavior that is not disruptive or escalating include restitution and loss of privileges (Jones & Downing, 1991; Swanson & Richard, 1993).

Time-out is widely endorsed in the behavior modification literature as a temporary respite measure (Murray & Sefchik, 1992). For time-out to be effective, however, the broader context must be highly reinforcing (Jones & Downing, 1991). Also, to be used safely and ethically, time-out should be used only within the context of a comprehensive behavior management system that also includes positive reinforcement for appropriate behavior and that limits the length of time allowed a child or adolescent to regain control. Residents in time-out need to be monitored closely, and rooms used for time-out must meet appropriate safety standards. After resolution of the inappropriate behavior, residents should be engaged in verbal processing of the episode, a process that has been referred to as remediation or debriefing (Kuster et al., 1988). This debriefing should attempt to help the resident accept responsibility for the problem behavior and verify that the resident understands why the inappropriate behavior was unacceptable, what the antecedents were, and what alternative responses could be made in future similar circumstances. After remediation, the resident needs to be reintroduced to the group with sensitivity to minimize embarrassment or humiliation (Murray & Sefchik, 1992).

Murray and Sefchik (1992) have proposed model licensing requirements to assist licensing agencies in regulating behavior management practices in children's residential facilities. They specifically propose prohibitions against certain aversive practices they do not consider justifiable according to empirical research on use of these procedures with emotionally disturbed and/or assaultive youth. Practices they would prohibit include forced physical exercise as a consequence contingent on misbehavior and group punishment, or "group contingency," for an individual's misbehavior. Murray and Sefchik also underscore the importance of using positive reinforcement and, along with Durrant (1993), emphasize that consequences for inappropriate behavior should have instructive rather than simply punitive value.

CRISIS INTERVENTION

Seclusion and Restraint

The physical environment, therapeutic milieu, and policies governing standard behavioral interventions should be designed, in part, to prevent crises from developing. Despite these safeguards, however, crises do occur, with the most dangerous involving accidental injury, runaway attempts, and suicidal and assaultive behaviors. In all of these situations, the immediate and overriding consideration is to protect the well-being of all clients at risk of harm. This may involve, at times, restraining or isolating clients to help prevent injury and to help them regain self-control.

In many inpatient and residential settings, seclusion refers to placing a child or adolescent in locked isolation.[1] The rationale for using seclusion varies somewhat with setting and discipline (Fassler & Cotton, 1992; Goren & Curtis, 1995; Miller, Walker, & Friedman, 1989; Tsemberis & Sullivan, 1988), but seclusion is usually intended to contain dangerous or potentially dangerous acting-out when less intrusive methods are ineffective or not feasible. Seclusion should not be used as punishment, to prevent runaways, for staff convenience, or because of understaffing (Brown & Tooke, 1992; Fassler & Cotton, 1992; Murray & Sefchik, 1992).

In psychiatric contexts, seclusion traditionally has been viewed as therapeutic in that it contains a dangerous situation and reduces sensory stimulation to patients while isolating them from unpleasant interactions or situations (Wherry, 1986). The containment is thought to reassure patients, and the sensory reduction and isolation to provide relief. In theory, seclusion reduces patients' distress and enables them to regain self-control more readily (Gutheil, 1978, in Fassler & Cotton, 1992). Seclusion thereby presumably reduces the need for chemical restraint (i.e., sedating medication) or mechanical restraint (such as leather restraints securing a patient's extremities and trunk to a bed). Some proponents of seclusion have assumed that, over time, seclusion will decrease a patient's dangerous acting-out.

Cotton (1989) and her colleagues have been particularly articulate proponents of seclusion as a therapeutic intervention for children. Building on the work of Gutheil (1978, in Cotton, 1989, and Fassler & Cotton, 1992) with adults and viewing children's development in psychodynamic terms, Cotton identifies containment, isolation, and a decrease in sensory input as important functions of seclusion with children, particularly when viewed within a developmental context that recognizes the ego deficits exhibited by children referred for inpatient treatment. Millstein and Cotton (1990) examined 102 children admitted to a child psychiatric unit and discovered that those most prone to being secluded were more likely to also have histories of physical abuse, assaultive behavior, and a suicide attempt within the 6 months prior to admission; neurological impairment; poorer verbal ability; and coping skills deficits including behavioral rigidity, impulsivity, failure to understand behavioral expectations, difficulty accepting external control, and poor frustration tolerance.[2] Cotton (1989) sees such children as typically "relationship-resistant," unable to learn from their mistakes, unable to rely on others, and apt to confuse discipline by staff with retaliatory punishment they have experienced in the past. Their need for seclusion, she maintains, reflects their distress. She believes seclusion can enhance their sense of safety, prevent their escalation into increasingly dangerous behavior, and help them begin to learn basic coping skills.

Seclusion is a controversial intervention, however, that poses a risk of physical injury for both patient and staff (Blair, 1991). Also, research is raising questions about its presumed therapeutic benefits (Angold & Pickles, 1993; Brown & Tooke, 1992; Goren et al., 1993; Goren et al., in press; Miller, 1986; Tsemberis & Sullivan, 1988). Goren et al. (1993; Goren et al., in press) have found, for example, that clients' acting-out tends to either not improve or worsen when seclusion is employed.

Others have found that the repetition of seclusion for adolescent and
child patients does not necessarily shorten the duration of those patients' seclusions (Angold & Pickles, 1993). One report has indicated
that introducing a seclusion room into a children's inpatient unit did not
result in fewer straightjacket orders; seclusion was simply added to the
staff's repertoire of patient management interventions (Tsemberis &
Sullivan, 1988). Staff of a child psychiatric inpatient unit and at a
residential center have reported successful operation without the use of
seclusion (Irwin, 1987; Miller, 1986). Miller (1986) has documented
seclusion's potentially detrimental effects from the child's point-of-
view by asking residents ages 5 to 13 in residential treatment to draw
and write about seclusion. The results suggest children perceive seclusion as a punitive, often frightening isolation.

Goren et al. (1993; Goren et al., in press) argue that seclusion is a
coercive response to patient aggression that often reinforces the patient's aggression. Drawing upon Patterson's (1976) research demon-
strating how children and adolescents can learn to be oppositional and
aggressive in response to coercive parenting, she describes how youngsters carry their oppositional, aggressive style into treatment settings
and evoke coercive responses from staff. When staff respond coer-
cively, the cycle gets perpetuated and the pattern is reinforced for the
patient.

Seclusion has also been criticized on ethical and legal grounds. Smith
(1991) considers seclusion a form of involuntary confinement with
potential for child abuse and, along with Wherry (1986), clearly delineates it as a psychiatric treatment or management strategy, not a behavior
modification technique. Smith (1991) argues that seclusion may be used
only when clinically justified (in cases of imminently dangerous or
severely deteriorating behavior); when voluntary informed consent is
given by the youth (depending on age), parent, or guardian; when
properly planned and supervised; and when due process including
referral to a grievance panel is provided for children and parents or
guardians. Informed consent involves youths, or their guardians in case
of minors, understanding all that is involved in a treatment procedure,
including possible side effects, and acting without duress in giving
permission for use of the procedure. Because youngsters and their
parents or other guardians are often under some duress when the child
is being placed in a hospital or residential facility, it is difficult at times
to ensure that the consent is being given voluntarily. Informed consent
can be approximated, however, if staff explain fully to youths and their

guardians how restrictive behavior management strategies are used. Family and guardians also need to be informed when these practices have been instituted with their child and how their child responded. The use of these procedures needs to be reviewed systematically, such as through peer review or human rights committees (Murray & Sefchik, 1992).

Wherry (1986) does not advocate the use of seclusion because it is a high-risk procedure with potential adverse effects for staff as well as patients. He recognizes, however, that seclusion is sometimes necessary for safety reasons and provides guidelines for its therapeutic implementation. First, he advocates that seclusion be viewed as a process rather than a singular event, and that staff be trained in managing the preceding events and aftermath, as well as the seclusion itself, therapeutically. He advises that staff, while executing the seclusion, give the resident calming messages, avoid confrontational messages, monitor their own feelings, remove patients' articles of clothing or contents of pockets that could pose a threat for self-injury, and intervene to prevent harm in cases of attempted self-injury. Wherry also suggests that staff remain with the patient when it appears their presence is reassuring rather than antagonizing. Similar recommendations have been made by others. Cotton (1989; Fassler & Cotton, 1992) discusses the importance of seclusion being viewed as a process that reduces demands on an overwhelmed child and minimizes any detrimental aspects. She recommends that seclusion rooms be made attractive and comfortable and allow children to remain in contact with people (e.g., by being able to look through a window into a staff member's office). She echoes Wherry's points that staff must respond in a firm but caring and reassuring manner.

Restraint as an intervention method is often paired with seclusion in the research and clinical literature. In hospital settings, restraint usually refers to the use of either mechanical or chemical restraints, although a form of "therapeutic holding" that involves immobilization of the patient's limbs has also been reported (Miller et al., 1989). The use of mechanical restraints is ordered by a physician and is typically restricted to implementation in settings in which medical staff trained in mechanical restraint carry out the procedure. Mechanical restraints include, with younger children, the use of a papoose board (with the child being swaddled against a board with canvas restraints) and, with children and adolescents, securing the patient's extremities with straps while the patient lies in bed. Other forms of mechanical restraint include the straightjacket (which allows ambulation but restricts the arms), the body bag (which zips to enclose the patient's body from the neck down, thus immobilizing the patient), and swaddling in blankets. Murray and Sefchik (1992) recommend soft leather restraints or handcuffs as the preferred method for mechanical restraint, and suggest certain types of restraints should be prohibited, including leg irons, straightjackets, papoose boards, ropes, metal and Teflon handcuffs, body wraps, body tubes, blanketing, and four/five point restraint.

Legal and ethical challenges to the use of mechanical and chemical restraints have been made (Miller et al., 1989), and some mental health professionals argue against the use of all forms of restraint with preadolescents (Masters & Devany, 1992). Masters and Devany (1992) voice concerns, for example, that even manual restraint of children during tantrums risks the child confusing aggression with being held lovingly. When mechanical and chemical restraints are used, stringent safeguards to ensure patients' safety are necessary. These include only trained staff implementing mechanical restraint (e.g., see Mazzarins, Payne, & Kupfersmid, 1988, for guidelines), staff observing the youth at all times during restraint, and medical staff checking the youth for possible injury after termination of a restraint (Murray & Sefchik, 1992).

Outside of medical settings, the use of restraint is typically limited to various approved forms of physical holding, such as the baskethold restraint (in which a staff member, from behind the client, holds the client's arms crossed across the client's body). A physical hold, or physical escort, is also used to move patients when necessary (e.g., when they will not voluntarily move into a seclusion room). Hurting or potentially harming the resident in any way (e.g., by kneeling or sitting on the chest or back) is not acceptable (Murray & Sefchik, 1992). Wherry (1986) has provided these guidelines for effective physical restraints:

> (a) implementation in the context of an ongoing relationship between staff and patient; (b) identification of staff feelings before, during, and after restraint; (c) awareness and identification of potential feelings elicited in the patient; (d) thorough planning including removal of other patients, anticipating consequences, having enough staff, and gaining control cleanly; (e) calm communication by one staff member . . .; (f) determination of when the patient can be released gradually; and (g) continuation of the therapeutic process once the patient is released (including discussion of factors precipitating the crisis and future alternative solutions). (pp. 58-59)

The standard of care that seems to be emerging in the field, and that appears consistent with relevant legal decisions (Brown & Tooke, 1992), is that seclusion and restraint should be considered crisis management strategies employed as a last resort to prevent harm when other, less intrusive methods have failed to avert the crisis. The intervention may serve to protect either the client, in the case of self-injury, and/or staff or other patients being aggressed against (Kuster et al., 1988; Swanson & Richard, 1993; Thomas, 1982). The use of seclusion or mechanical, chemical, or prolonged physical restraint is seen as justifiable, if at all, only to prevent harm. After the client calms down and becomes responsive to verbal intervention, processing the episode with on-line staff and in therapy may help minimize some of the countertherapeutic effects of the intervention and help the patient learn more adaptive, alternative coping or communication skills. Each episode of restraint or seclusion should be documented in an incident report, along with documentation that other, less restrictive interventions had been attempted first. Alternative treatment strategies should be explored for future interventions, especially when restraint or seclusion proves ineffective or aggravating to a resident's behavior (Brown & Tooke, 1992; Fassler & Cotton, 1992; Murray & Sefchik, 1992).

Another important standard of care is that every effort should be made to prevent seclusion or restraint becoming necessary with patients or residents (Blair, 1991; Blair & New, 1991; Goren et al., 1994; Irwin, 1987; Mercer, 1982; Miller, 1986; Miller et al., 1989; Rindfleisch & Baros-Van Hull, 1982; Titus, 1989). Some risk factors (e.g., patient diagnosis and history of assault) cannot be modified, but others can. The therapeutic environment can be structured to minimize unnecessary demands and frustrations, and staff can be taught to set limits in therapeutic ways (e.g., by posing choices for residents that emphasize potential benefits to be gained). Staff can be helped to develop nonauthoritarian, patient-centered attitudes; to be active listeners and facilitators of problem solving; and to resolve any conflicts they might have with peers or their charges. Administration can ensure adequate staffing, effective leadership, support for on-line staff, and training and policies that take the risk of staff as well as client injury seriously. Staff particularly need to learn nonintrusive intervention methods, such as verbal deescalation, for use early in the sequence of client behaviors apt to escalate into dangerous or destructive behavior. Administrators also can make a serious commitment to review each instance of the use of seclusion or restraint and to involve parents, agency representatives, and other members of the community in the center's programs.

Although direct care staff working with children and adolescents need training in the safe and ethical use of seclusion and restraint, mental health professionals also need education and training in the uses of these procedures and in the implications for staff and clients of their use. There is also a real need for more research and clarity in terminology relevant to seclusion and restraint practices (Crespi, 1990; Fassler & Cotton, 1992). Few relevant empirical studies have been conducted and, despite their widespread, long-standing, and controversial use, seclusion and restraint are employed in the absence of much consensus regarding their implementation. As of 1985, there was not even majority agreement nationwide about whether time-out and seclusion should be distinguished (American Psychiatric Association, 1985, in Crespi, 1990).

Suicide Prevention

Comprehensive suicide prevention programs are necessary in inpatient and residential treatment settings serving child and adolescent patients. These patients as a group are at higher risk for suicide than the general population of their peers, and specific individuals may be immediate, extreme risks. Key preventive elements include a physical environment, staffing and supervisory practices, and behavior policies that minimize risk factors; individualized treatment planning that can be modified as needed to accommodate varying degrees of suicidal behavior; and on-line staff trained in identifying possible indicators of suicide risk and responding therapeutically to suicidal behavior.

Accrediting agencies typically specify requirements for safety in the physical plant, and standards may include such precautions as safety glass in windows and doors, locked covers on electrical outlets, restrictive window openings, and locked doors in specified areas. Layout of physical spaces such as corridors and common rooms should allow ready observation for supervision by staff. Other safety precautions include breakaway shower and clothes rods and shields over lighting fixtures. When specific individuals are deemed at risk, they may be placed on a restrictive status that includes further alteration of their physical environment, depending on the imminence and severity of threat involved. They may not be permitted, for example, to wear belts or shoe laces and may have continual one-on-one observation by staff. Behavior policies that may reduce risk for suicide include those that limit children's access to unsupervised areas and potential weapons. Staff should be adequately trained and supervised, and all relevant staff observations, decisions, and actions should be clearly communicated and documented (James & Wherry, 1991). The staff-to-client ratio must permit adequate supervision of all children and adolescents, especially those deemed at risk of self-injury or suicide.

Treatment planning for potentially suicidal youth begins with assessment of referral and intake information by clinical staff expert in the clinical and empirical literature on suicide among children and adolescents. Clients not deemed at risk for suicide at admission might be referred later for reevaluation if staff observe behavior suggestive of increased risk. Risk factors include a history of suicidal behavior or threats, including any recent, serious suicidal attempt or current suicidal ideation and intention; presence of an affective disorder or psychosis; feelings of hopelessness, worthlessness, intense unresolved anger, or being overwhelmed and out of control; significant losses, emotional deprivation, and social isolation (e.g., death of a parent or other significant person, family disorganization or dissolution, rejection or abandonment by parents, multiple home placements, alienation from family or peers, recent break-up of a love relationship, recent significant loss of self-esteem); trauma, including abuse and repeated hospitalizations; affective disorder, other significant psychopathology, and proclivity to violence in the family; suicidal behavior or completed suicide among family or friends—or a person/character recently publicized in the media; and alcohol or other drug abuse by the youth or his or her parents. Evaluation of the youngster should include examination of the youth's understanding of and motivation to die; identification of both predisposing and mitigating factors; assessment of the lethality and specificity of any suicide plans the youth might have developed; and examination of the youngster's access to the means to carry out a plan (Braga, 1989; Charles & Matheson, 1991; James & Wherry, 1991; Maas & Ney, 1992; Pfeffer, 1989; Slaby & McGuire, 1989).

Staff need to be alert for not only youths' direct expressions of a wish to harm themselves or die but also for indirect signs such as musings about life after death, vague references to death in conversation or written materials, and excessive accident-prone behavior. Staff should also report changes in usual affect and behavior, especially prolonged depressions (particularly if followed inexplicably by a manic-like positive mood), increased anger and impulsiveness, disturbances in eating and sleep patterns, withdrawal from usual activities or friends, being

more preoccupied or distracted than usual, decreased school performance, decreased interest in appearance and hygiene, excessive fatigue
or somatic complaints, and giving away prized possessions (Braga,
1989; Charles & Matheson, 1991; James & Wherry, 1991; Maas & Ney,
1992; Slaby & McGuire, 1989). Braga (1989) has developed a protocol
to guide clinicians and treatment teams through a systematic risk assessment, including evaluation of behavioral patterns that on-line staff
may observe.

Protective measures must be taken immediately when a child or
adolescent is deemed an acute, serious risk for suicide. These cases
include, according to Braga (1989), "the adolescent with a past history
of several losses, multiple placements, lack of a sense of belonging in
a nuclear family, who is filled with anger and hatred and who may
entertain fantasies of future revenge against significant others" (pp.
14-15) and psychotic children or adolescents experiencing command
hallucinations to kill themselves. Youths considered at imminent risk
for engaging in potentially lethal behavior are typically referred to
inpatient psychiatric settings because these are typically the most secure facilities and are more highly staffed than other treatment programs by mental health professionals, including psychiatrists. Youths
who actually harm themselves, of course, require medical attention
appropriate to the type and degree of injury involved.

Less extreme suicide risks may be maintained in residential treatment
settings having adequate environmental safeguards, intervention plans,
and trained staff. Suicidal behavior ranges along a continuum of severity,
identified by James and Wherry (1991), from a suicidal tendency through
suicidal gestures and threats to a suicidal attempt and, if completed,
suicide. Degree of suicide risk needs to be assessed in terms of this
continuum, and type of intervention should be related to assessed level of
risk. Youths deemed at mild risk, for example, should be observed more
closely than usual. Those at higher risk might require transfer to a more
secure setting or restriction from certain activities and constant observation
one-on-one by staff (Braga, 1989). Manipulative or attention-seeking
suicidal comments and behaviors need to be distinguished (but not over-
looked or ignored as the distress messages they typically represent) from
more seriously suicidal behavior. Parents or guardians need to be notified
whenever their children exhibit suicidal behavior and informed fully
regarding protective and treatment interventions taken.

Staff communication with suicidal clients needs to be supportive and
oriented toward helping the client cope with the immediate crisis (e.g.,

by expanding his or her constricted thinking and developing hope of change). Helpful strategies include iterating options and alternative solutions to current problems (James & Wherry, 1991; Slaby & McGuire, 1989). Other useful interventions suggested by James and Wherry (1991) include "self-esteem building, dealing with negative thoughts, cognitive restructuring, self-monitoring, confidence training, relaxation training, contracting, . . . increasing activity levels, [and] . . . involving the family" (p. 31). They recommend that staff not belittle, criticize, moralize, show panic, focus unduly on the suicidal behavior, or make unrealistic promises.

Some patients will harm themselves significantly, and some will successfully complete suicide in inpatient and residential settings. These events represent a crisis not only for the patient's family but also for the patient's peers in treatment and for staff. Besides attending to the suicide survivor, immediate actions taken should include support for the family, stabilization of the unit (including providing support for peers), and support for staff (James & Wherry, 1991; Maas & Ney, 1992). Longer term resolution on the unit will involve processing the events with staff and patients to facilitate emotional and intellectual resolution and planning toward prevention of recurrences of the acts (Maas & Ney, 1992).

Sequelae of Abuse

Many children and adolescents in residence in treatment centers have histories of physical, emotional, and/or sexual abuse. The sequelae of abuse encompass a broad range of psychopathology that need to be addressed in treatment (Famularo, Kinscherff, & Fenton, 1990; Saigh, 1989) in both the day-to-day therapeutic milieu (Swanson & Richard, 1993) and in specialized forms of treatment, such as group therapy for children experiencing posttraumatic stress disorder (Doyle & Bauer, 1989) and/or surviving sexual abuse (Zahn, 1991). The sequelae of abuse pose crises for staff most often when the residents become self-destructive (Barber et al., 1994), as discussed above, or perpetrate abuse upon others (Small et al., 1991).

The clinical literature has documented the increased risk of potentially abusive acting-out exhibited by victims of abuse (Johnson, 1988, 1989), and a few empirical studies specifically targeting youths in residential treatment are beginning to appear. Johnson and Aoki (1993), for example, have demonstrated in a study of latency-age children in nine nonrandomly selected residential treatment centers that these children exhibit a high rate of sexual behavior. Some of the sexual behavior is "natural and expectable" (e.g., talks about sex with friends, shows interest in sex differences), and some is more problematic or clearly pathological (e.g., tries to touch "private parts" of adults or children, tries to place mouth on or penis in others' "private parts"). On two different measures of sexual behavior, Johnson and Aoki (1993) discovered that children who had been both physically and sexually abused (the majority of their sample) were especially prone to exhibit sexual behavior. Presumably, the risk for sexual acting-out is even greater with adolescents, who comprise some 70% of residential treatment centers' populations (Aldgate, 1987, in Braga, 1993).

A comprehensive program addressing youths' sexual behaviors will (a) include environmental and programmatic measures to prevent clients being victimized by other clients; (b) provide for nurturing physical contact between client and caregiver (e.g., appropriate hugs) and otherwise promote healthy sexual development in all clients; and (c) provide individualized treatment plans and therapy to address the sexual acting-out of patients. Safety measures include assigning children and adolescents with known histories of sexual acting-out or highly sexualized behavior to single bedrooms, allowing only one youth at a time in bathrooms, securing difficult-to-supervise spaces, and supervising youths closely (e.g., at approximately 15-minute intervals throughout the night and when youths are in potentially high-risk situations such as playing alone with one other peer or with a younger child). Educational measures include teaching clients about respecting the limits of others' personal space and how to resist and report sexual advances by others. Latency-aged and, especially, adolescent patients should be involved in educational curricula that share sexual information in developmentally appropriate ways. Staff should be trained to neither deny nor normalize pathological acting-out, nor take repressive measures against developmentally normal sexual behaviors. Policies should provide clear guidelines for staff regarding supervision requirements and appropriate boundaries of staff-to-patient as well as patient-to-patient contact and interactions. Staff also need help clarifying their own values related to sexuality and addressing transference and countertransference issues that arise (Caldwell & Rejino, 1993; Crenshaw, 1993; Johnson & Aoki, 1993; Lambert, 1977; Nevin, 1993; Schimmer, 1993). Caldwell and Rejino (1993, p. 60) have developed checklists of environmental factors that clinicians and administrators need to consider when developing a comprehensive prevention program.

Treatment plans of sexually acting-out clients should address specific sexual behaviors to be targeted. Verbal interventions, rewards for appropriate behavior, and consequences for acting out should be specified for on-line staff working with the youth (Johnson & Aoki, 1993). Open, frank conversations about sexual behavior and any problems that arise should be the norm with both the acting-out youngsters and their peers. Distinguishing between normal sexual experimentation or play, sexualized behavior, and sexually abusive behavior can be accomplished if staff take into account the ages and social relationships of those involved (and any distinguishing pattern of characteristics associated with people chosen for sexual activity); the nature of the sexual contact and how it occurs (especially whether force or other coercion, deception, or intimidation are used); the persistence or progression of the contact; and any fantasies that accompany the sexual behavior (Gil, 1991, and Groth, 1977, in Braga, 1993). If a youth is identified as a perpetrator of sexual abuse, a treatment center must ensure the safety of those involved, report the molestation to proper authorities including monitoring agencies, refer clients for medical services as indicated, inform parents or guardians, evaluate its ability to keep other youngsters safe while working with the perpetrator, and conduct an internal review to help prevent recurrences of such events. Perpetrators may need to be housed separately from other clients, will require very close supervision, and will require therapy focusing specifically on sexually aggressive behavior. Victims will need special support because client-to-client sexual abuse can have serious consequences (Braga, 1993; Caldwell & Rejino, 1993; Johnson & Aoki, 1993).

WELL-TRAINED STAFF

Murray and Sefchik (1992) have asserted that strong training requirements for on-line staff are the single most effective means of ensuring the safety and therapeutic treatment of youth in residential settings. Staff who work directly with residents have highly demanding, stressful roles, and, compared to other staff in the facility, often have little relevant training or education for their positions. A strong in-service program is essential to ensuring that the staff have the skills and confidence necessary to function effectively (Blair, 1991; Colyar, 1991; Corcoran, 1993; Doyle & Bauer, 1989; Kagan, 1993; Nevin, 1993). On-line staff particularly need to understand why youth act out, how to deescalate volatile situations, how to manage aggressive behavior and other crises, and how to work together as a cohesive team (Katz, 1993; Lambert, 1977). Observation of skilled staff on the job, perhaps being paired with a mentor, and supervised practice in nonphysical as well as physical interventions are necessary. Administrative support for a thorough orientation, further subsequent training, and ongoing supervision is critical (Blair, 1991; Colyar, 1991; Mercer, 1982; Murray & Sefchik, 1992).

SUMMARY

The treatment milieu is a critical therapeutic element in both inpatient and residential settings. It should provide adaptive and corrective experiences and, for the severely disturbed child or adolescent who lacks adequate self-control, much external structure and control. As youngsters develop greater self-regulatory capacities, the external supports and constraints should be systematically relaxed. External control is often provided in the form of structured, predictable, daily routines and consistently enforced rules and behavioral limits. Treatment programming should be flexible enough, however, to accommodate individual residents' needs, strengths, interests, and cultural backgrounds, and should be as normal as possible to help prevent institutionalization of youngsters. Parents and other family members should be encouraged to participate in treatment, and youngsters should have experiences and relationships outside the treatment facility.

An important component of a therapeutic environment is a comprehensive behavior management program that emphasizes positive and supportive interventions, therapeutic communication, and trust-inspiring relationships between staff and their charges. Youngsters' strengths and emerging abilities should be fostered within the context of a nurturing, reinforcing environment. Positive reinforcements may be awarded in the form of privileges and treats that youngsters earn by achieving behavioral goals.

Behavior problems should be managed with the least intrusive interventions possible, and more intrusive, especially aversive, interventions should be allowed only when clearly justified and according to carefully conceived, explicit policy. Some problem behaviors may be safely ignored and eliminated through extinction; others may be successfully redirected, reframed, or modified through problem solving, paradoxical intention or other noncoercive, nonpunitive strategies. Exclusionary and nonexclusionary time-outs, followed by debriefing, often help interrupt disruptive behavioral escalations. More discrete, controlled behavior problems may be solved effectively with restitution, room restrictions for predetermined lengths of time, or loss of specific privileges. The use of such aversive consequences should have instructive rather than simply punitive value.

Staff must be selected and supervised carefully, and they should be trained to cope effectively during crises and with oppositional and manipulative youngsters. Some of the more common and dangerous crises include youngsters' violent acting-out, suicidal and self-injurious behaviors, and sexual exploitation of peers. Staff should be trained to identify risk factors, seek consultation as needed, and correctly implement and document use of emergency procedures such as restraint or seclusion of a combative youth or supervising a youngster deemed at risk of suicide. Administrators must develop policies, procedures, and support systems that emphasize prevention of dangerous acting-out and the implementation of protective measures immediately whenever such acting-out occurs.

To be therapeutic, treatment settings must provide for youngsters' physical and psychological safety and guarantee their legal, ethical, and humanitarian rights. Specific rights include those guaranteeing protection, sustenance, freedom from undue invasion of privacy, access to family and friends, respect for one's cultural and religious values, confidentiality, and treatment and other services that foster developmental progress.

NOTES

1. Fassler and Cotton's (1992) national survey of seclusion practices indicates great variability in the definition of seclusion, however, with this definition representing the conservative extreme and the removal of a youngster from a group to any designated space representing the broadest definition.

2. Angold and Pickles (1993) have criticized the statistical analyses employed in studies in which repeated incidents of seclusion for particular children are treated as independent observations. Their own analyses of seclusion of adolescents indicated, with respect to client characteristics, that only age correlated with frequency of seclusion (younger clients being secluded more often) and that age and psychotic status interacted to predict duration of seclusion (with younger nonpsychotics being secluded for shorter periods).

4

EVALUATING THE EFFECTIVENESS OF RESIDENTIAL AND INPATIENT TREATMENT

Evaluating the effectiveness of residential and inpatient treatment programs for children and adolescents is an extremely complex but very important task. As discussed in Chapter 1, these programs are limited in capacity and require the commitment of inordinate quantities of financial and personnel resources to operate. Therefore, ineffective operation of such "deep-end" programs can impair the efficiency of the entire continuum of mental health treatment.

There are a number of methodological issues that are critical in the evaluation of residential and inpatient programs for children and adolescents. Wilson and Lyman (1983) state that there are five critical aspects to the evaluation of such programs. These elements will be discussed here, after which the literature on the effectiveness of residential and inpatient programs will be briefly reviewed.

DEFINITION AND MEASUREMENT OF OUTCOME

One of the most fundamental concerns of evaluative research in this area is the definition and measurement of outcome. Wilson and Lyman (1983) make six recommendations concerning the outcome evaluation of residential and inpatient treatment programs:

1. Outcome should be conceptualized and measured as multidimensional and multidirectional, and outcome/evaluation measures should be designed to assess both positive and negative changes in a variety of behavioral and/or adjustment areas.

2. Programs should use standardized, objective outcome measures to allow for both internal and external comparability of data and to reduce the influence of such threats to evaluative integrity as "criterion drift" and "self-justifying assessment."

3. Programs should attend to the concerns raised by Emery and Marholin (1977) regarding the social irrelevance of many outcome measures selected for assessment. Residential treatment programs tend to select for scrutiny behaviors that are unique to such treatment environments, and, although troublesome during a child's treatment, they may disappear or become irrelevant to adjustment after discharge. Another aspect of this issue is the need for evaluative research to include measures of functioning/ adjustment after discharge and return to the child's natural environment, rather than terminating assessment at the time of discharge. The inclusion of follow-up assessment allows conclusions to be drawn concerning the generalizability of treatment effects.

4. As mentioned by Margolis, Sorensen, and Galano (1977), residential and inpatient treatment programs should include measures of consumer satisfaction in their outcome assessment. Implementation of such an action would require careful consideration of the question, "Who are the consumers of the program's services?" and would probably result in a broadened application of such measures to include referral and community social service agencies, families of clients, and children in treatment themselves.

5. Outcome evaluation should acknowledge that maturational and developmental changes occur in children and that measures and evaluation design should allow for the separation of treatment effects from changes that are solely due to maturation or developmental changes.

6. Outcome measures should acknowledge the possible nonlinearity of change, and evaluation design should allow the temporal pattern of such change to be explored, as well as explicate the relationship between different components of treatment and outcome.

In addition to these six areas of concern, Wilson and Lyman (1983) also emphasize the point that outcome must always be evaluated in terms of cost of treatment, whether this cost is defined in monetary terms or in terms of psychosocial cost to the client and his or her family.

DEFINING AND MEASURING TREATMENT

A significant weakness in much of the research literature on the effectiveness of residential and inpatient treatment is its failure to adequately specify or independently verify components of treatment

(Wodarski, Feldman, & Pedi, 1974). Researchers tend to consider the treatment provided by residential and inpatient providers to be self-evident and often fail to provide enough detail to allow replication of the treatment approach. Such labels as "a therapeutic community", or "a comprehensive, levels-based contingency management program" simply do not provide enough information to allow causal links between intervention and outcome to be hypothesized. The number of possibly active therapeutic variables in operation in a residential or inpatient treatment program is extremely large, and researchers need to specifically define and operationalize a large enough number of these so that replication can establish which are the truly therapeutic elements. Many programs have mistakenly attributed their treatment success to (or conversely, blamed a lack of success on) program elements that subsequent research has shown to be irrelevant to outcome. A failure to define treatment elements specifically enough to allow such subsequent evaluation research to be done will doom programs to guesswork in their efforts to refine and improve their treatment programs. A similar cognitive error is the mistake of thinking that the totality of the residential treatment environment is indivisible and that it is impossible to explicate subcomponents of this environment. Such thinking leads to the mindless replication of "successful" treatment models even if some expensive and restrictive elements of these models contribute little to their treatment efficacy (or even reduce it).

An additional shortcoming in much of the evaluation research on residential and inpatient treatment is its failure to document treatment implementation. Often, evaluation studies describe treatment components in an idealized way and offer no proof that actual implementation approaches this standard. Anyone who has worked in residential or inpatient treatment environments knows that the way in which even carefully defined treatment procedures are implemented by weekend and night staff who are not being observed is often very different from their description on the treatment plan. Evaluation research that fails to acknowledge and provide measurement of this difference runs the risk of underestimating the effectiveness of properly implemented treatment procedures. Even research that purports to assess the degree of treatment implementation may fail to accomplish this goal adequately. Scheirer and Rezmovic (1983) surveyed 74 research studies that incorporated some measure of treatment implementation into their design and concluded that the vast majority of the measures used were inadequate to establish whether or not appropriate implementation had occurred.

RESEARCH DESIGN

The design of evaluation research provides the framework for interpreting, understanding, and using outcome data and determining possible relationships with treatment. Many purported evaluations of residential and inpatient treatment have no identifiable design beyond the reporting of some measure taken after treatment has terminated. It has been difficult to find anything approximating classical experimental design with random assignment, blind raters, and control groups. Additional problems include the use of different measures or different raters for pre- and posttreatment evaluations and the use of rating instruments with such low reliability that results are uninterpretable.

More recently, residential and inpatient treatment evaluation research has appeared in the literature that uses more sophisticated research designs such as single-subject, quasi-experimental, and multivariate approaches, and there now exists a body of literature with more interpretable results. The results of many of these studies will be discussed later in this chapter. One problem with the use of research designs using complicated statistical analyses is that the subject numbers available within any one program at a given time are usually quite modest, and some analyses require large numbers of subjects to reach minimal standards of validity. The answer to this dilemma is to collect data across time or across multiple service sites. Both of these approaches are problematic. Often, both treatment approaches and research and clinical personnel are far from static in residential and inpatient programs, and evaluation projects that continue for too long risk invalidation because of changes in treatment variables or discontinuation because of loss of a sponsor. Similarly, it is difficult to conduct multisite research because of an absence of standardized treatment models and outcome measures.

CHILD AND FAMILY CHARACTERISTICS

In addition to outcome, treatment, and design considerations, it would be useful if more evaluations of residential and inpatient treatment included child and family characteristics as independent or predictor variables. There is limited utility (and potential misinformation) in conducting evaluation research that yields results that are reported and interpretable only on the level of simple main effects (children who have been in residential treatment are doing better than those who did not receive such treatment) when the reality is at the level of a complicated interaction effect (some children from some families who receive some elements of residential treatment are doing better than some children who did not receive such treatment). Research that addresses these interactions contributes far more to our understanding of the effects of residential and inpatient treatment than does research that oversimplifies and distorts its results.

SELECTIVE REVIEW OF
THE RESIDENTIAL AND INPATIENT
TREATMENT EVALUATION LITERATURE

The following is a selective review of the literature on the effectiveness of residential and inpatient treatment. Space prevents a discussion of all evaluation research that has been published. Research has been selected for discussion here because of its historical significance, the frequency with which it is cited, the importance of its results, or because of methodological issues that it helps to illustrate. This review is generally organized chronologically (with some exceptions) to provide a historical perspective and to highlight changes in methodology and results over the years. Although all articles reviewed are concerned with treatment in residential treatment centers, inpatient hospitals, and juvenile correctional facilities, because of the imprecision of these labels no effort has been made to compare results between treatment settings or to group studies by this variable. Readers are referred to one of several comprehensive reviews of the residential and inpatient treatment literature that have been published in the past decade or so for articles that are not discussed here (Curry, 1991; Quay, 1986; Whittaker & Pecora, 1984; Wilson & Lyman, 1983).

Probably the first evaluation of the effectiveness of residential treatment for children and adolescents was published by Rosenthal and Pinsky in 1936. They reported on the status of 1,184 cases that had been discharged from The Child Guidance Home of Cincinnati and were either active or inactive in follow-up. They found that 62% of the active cases and 63% of the inactive cases were rated as "adjusted" rather than "unadjusted." Poorly defined terms and methodology render these results largely uninterpretable.

Another of the first evaluations of inpatient treatment for emotionally disturbed adolescents was offered by Beskind (1962). In this article, three studies were reviewed, and ratings of globally improved clinical status at discharge and follow-up were reported. Youngsters with neurotic or affective disorders were reported as having the highest rates of improvement (approximately 87%), whereas only about half of those with "psychopathic personality" were rated as improved at discharge. More than half of the adolescents diagnosed with schizophrenia were rated as improved at discharge, although this number declined significantly by the follow-up assessment. Typical for research of this era, there were no control groups, the outcome measure used was subjective and unsophisticated, and there was little attention given to the methodological concerns mentioned earlier in this chapter.

Craft, Stephenson, and Granger (1964) published a much more sophisticated early investigation of the effects of inpatient treatment on adolescent male "psychopaths." The subjects were treated with either a self-governing group therapy program or an "authoritarian" program, with both groups receiving monetary rewards based upon work performance and attitude. Assignment to the groups was random, and only subjects who remained in treatment for a minimum of 3 months were included in the data analysis. At discharge, the authoritarian group, but not the group therapy subjects, showed a statistically significant increase in IQ and a significant decrease in psychometrically measured impulsivity. Minnesota Multiphasic Personality Inventory profiles and social adjustment measures were unchanged for both groups. Follow-up interviews approximately 15 months after discharge found that although more than half of the subjects in each group had committed additional legal offenses, the subjects in the authoritarian group had committed significantly fewer than had the subjects in the group therapy group. In addition, only one fourth of the authoritarian boys were judged to be still in need of institutional care versus one half of the group therapy boys. Although this study has several significant methodological flaws, such as the absence of a control group and the use of potentially biased and subjective interview data, it is clearly more sophisticated and interesting than the studies reviewed by Beskind (1962).

An extremely influential early study of residential treatment outcome was conducted by Allerhand, Weber, and Haug (1966). The authors conducted discharge interviews and follow-up interviews 18 months later with 50 boys who had been in residential treatment for at least 6 months at Bellefaire in Ohio. Adjustment within the residential treatment environment was assessed at 3 and 15 months after admission through clinical records review. Results indicated that the boys' behavior improved during treatment but that this improvement did not correlate with adjustment at follow-up. Stress in the postdischarge environment appeared to be more predictive of follow-up adjustment. Overall, 71% of the boys were rated as functioning adequately at follow-up.

Hartmann, Glasser, Greenblatt, Soloman, and Levinson (1968) conducted a study of 55 adolescents who had been treated on an adult inpatient unit. A follow-up study (Herrera, Lifson, Hartmann, & Soloman, 1974) assessed these same youngsters' adjustment at 6 months, 1 year, 5 years, and 10 years after hospital discharge. Almost half of the sample was diagnosed as schizophrenic. After 10 years, 63% of the subjects were rated as improved over their status at admission, 15% were judged to be unchanged, and 27% were rated as worse. Only 42% were assessed as having fair or good adjustment, and half had been rehospitalized at some point. Only a few treatment variables were related to outcome, and these were confounded with severity of disorder. The absence of a control group and the subjective nature of the outcome measures reduce the meaningfulness of these results.

Anthony Davids and colleagues conducted two studies evaluating outcome for children treated at Bradley Hospital in Rhode Island, one of the first psychiatric hospitals for children in the United States. Davids, Ryan, and Salvatore (1968) assessed 27 males who received psychoanalytically oriented inpatient treatment for an average of 3.1 years between 1955 and 1964. Ten of the children were diagnosed as schizophrenic, and 17 were diagnosed as having "passive-aggressive personality." They found that approximately half of each diagnostic group had a good overall adjustment, but that an equal percentage (40% of schizophrenics, 47% of passive-aggressives) were institutionalized at the time of the follow-up. Children with better adjustment tended to be those with phobic behaviors, stubbornness, and those who were easily upset. No treatment variables were found that predicted outcome. Davids concluded in this article that "treatment variables (especially conventional psychotherapy) seem to bear little relationship to subsequent adjustment" (p. 474). The diagnoses of the children in this study appear somewhat suspect, and again the absence of a control group and adequate methodology diminish the interpretability and validity of the results.

In a later study, Davids and Salvatore (1976) assessed the outcome for 71 children who were in psychoanalytically oriented inpatient treatment for an average of 2 to 3 years at Bradley Hospital between 1953 and 1969. The children were diagnosed with passive-aggressive personality (41), schizoid personality (12), schizophrenia (11), and neurosis (7). A follow-up questionnaire was completed from 2 to 18 years after discharge. At follow-up, 41% of the subjects were rated as having good overall adjustment, 31% were rated as having fair adjustment, and 28% were rated as having poor adjustment. Most organismic and program variables appeared to be unrelated to outcome, although 3 (out of 21) referral problems predicted poor outcome: argumentativeness, lying, and "peculiar behavior or thinking." The prognosis given to the child at discharge was also found to be a poor predictor of outcome. Again, these results are difficult to interpret in the absence of a control group and with as much vagueness and subjectivity as exists in assessment procedures and measures.

Another early study was conducted by Monkman (1972) at an Illinois Department of Mental Health inpatient facility. Subjects were children between the ages of 7 and 13 who were experiencing emotional and adjustment difficulties. They varied widely in referral problems and intellectual capability, although severely psychotic children were excluded from the study. The children were exposed to a behavioral milieu therapy program that incorporated elements of contingency management and social skills training. Extensive behavioral data were collected while the children were in treatment and suggested that most children demonstrated a pattern of fewer problem behaviors and more socially appropriate behaviors over the course of their treatment (average duration of treatment was 8.3 months). Analysis of different interventions used during treatment indicated that "time-out" was generally more effective than response-cost interventions. Follow-up data obtained approximately 9 months after discharge through use of a questionnaire indicated that 55% of home-based problems and 53% of school-based problems were rated as improved, although only 27% of the home-based problems and 7% of the school-based were judged to be resolved to the point that they were indistinguishable from those of normal children. This early behavioral study lacked a control group, and the validity and sensitivity of the follow-up questionnaire is somewhat questionable, but this study is much more sophisticated, particularly in terms of the behavioral data gathered while children were in treatment, than much of the other evaluation research done during this same time period.

Taylor and Alpert (1973) conducted one of the seminal outcome evaluations of residential treatment. They assessed 75 children who had been treated at Children's Village for 6 months or longer and found that improvement during residential treatment was largely unrelated to postdischarge adjustment. Instead, they found that postdischarge adjustment was determined to a large extent by the amount of environmental and interpersonal support available in the postdischarge environment. This finding brings into question the fundamental and commonly held belief that behavior change effected within a residential treatment environment will, to a substantial degree, generalize to the postdischarge environment

Project Re-Ed (Hobbs, 1966) is a behaviorally oriented treatment approach that emphasizes reinforcement for socially appropriate behaviors and academic and social skills training. This model (originated at Cumberland House in Nashville, Tennessee) has spawned a network of treatment centers operating under a common philosophy called the Psychoeducational Model. The first outcome study done on Project Re-Ed was by Weinstein (1969, 1974). A sample of 122 boys between the ages of 6 and 12 who had behavioral problems and had been treated in Cumberland House for an average of 8.1 months served as subjects. In contrast to the earlier studies cited here, Weinstein constructed two control groups, one of 128 boys who had similar behavioral problems as the experimental group, and another of 128 boys without behavior problems. Behavioral ratings and psychological test data were obtained on the experimental group at the time of admission, at discharge, 6 months after discharge, and 18 months after discharge. Equivalent data were obtained for the two control groups at approximately the same time intervals. At discharge, 94% of treated children were rated as moderately or much improved by Re-Ed teachers, and 88% were rated as moderately or much improved by referral agencies. Test data indicated that treated children improved their self-concept, adopted a more internal locus of control, decreased in impulsivity, and perceived family relationships as more positive. Over the same time period, control subjects did not change in these attributes.

School behavior ratings at the 6-month and 18-month follow-ups indicated that 85% of the treated subjects maintained the progress they had shown at discharge and that, although both the treated group and the untreated behavior problem children had shown progress, the Re-Ed children had improved significantly more. At the 18-month follow-up, the Re-Ed children were rated as significantly less deviant than the untreated children. Ninety-two percent of Re-Ed children were rated as severely disturbed at admission, whereas only 44% were so rated at the

6-month follow-up and only 51% at the 18-month follow-up. For untreated, disturbed controls, the proportion rated severely disturbed was 91% at admission, 65% at 6-month follow-up, and 67% at 18-month follow-up. Academic improvement was significant from intake to the 18-month follow-up for the Re-Ed children but not for the untreated controls.

Another follow-up study was done on the Re-Ed program more recently (Lewis, 1988). Although this study found approximately the same overall rate of improvement as Weinstein's (1974) earlier research, the focus was really on identifying "ecological" predictors of postdischarge adjustment. Results suggested that personal data available at admission were not a good predictor of later adjustment, but that family socioeconomic status, family parenting behaviors, membership in a multiproblem family, and progress made by both children and families while the children were in residential treatment did predict later adjustment.

The outcome evaluation conducted by the Re-Ed program is a quantum leap ahead of that done by most residential treatment providers. The inclusion of control groups allows improvement to be attributed more clearly to the treatment program. Although the use of ratings rather than direct observation adds an element of subjectivity to the assessment, it still "might well serve as a model for the evaluation of residential treatment" (Quay, 1986, p. 569).

Jesness (1971) conducted an outcome evaluation study at a large California institution for delinquent male adolescents. Although at first glance such a facility might appear to have little in common with smaller residential treatment environments for emotionally disturbed children and adolescents, the overlap in problem behaviors and intervention strategies between the two classifications of facilities is substantial. Treatment in Jesness's study consisted of placement in a residential unit with a unique prescriptive treatment milieu based on the residents' delinquent typology as measured by the California I-level classification system (Warren, 1969). The control group consisted of youths assigned to a standard training school treatment milieu without regard to unique delinquent typology. The experimental group experienced fewer behavior problems during treatment; however, there was no differential impact on posttreatment adjustment, with 54% of each group committing parole violations during the first 15 months after discharge and 64% of each group committing violations in the first 24 months after discharge. Thus, not only did this study fail to demonstrate an advantage to prescriptive, individualized residential treatment for delinquent youth, it also emphasized the ineffectiveness of traditional institutional treatment for such youth.

Another, later study by Jesness (1975) contrasted an institutional treatment program for delinquent youth based on transactional analysis group sessions with a program based on contingency management and behavioral contracting. Although there were a number of psychometric differences between the two groups, they did not differ in the percentage of youths committing parole violations in the first 24 months following discharge. In each group, approximately 47% of the subjects violated parole. The rate of parole violations at 1 year, however, was lower for both programs than it had been for the previous 2 years under a traditional training school treatment model. The rate was also lower than for two other juvenile correctional institutions with equivalent populations. It is hard to be very encouraged, however, by a recidivism rate approaching 50%.

Another residential treatment model for delinquent or conduct-disordered youth that has generated a significant quantity of outcome research is the Teaching Family Model, which originated at the Achievement Place group home in Kansas in the late 1960s and has since been replicated at more than 200 sites nationwide. The program is a behavioral one, with a comprehensive point and level system in which appropriate behavior earns privileges and inappropriate behavior results in a loss of privilege. A number of publications (e.g., Kifer, Lewis, Green, & Phillips, 1974; Phillips et al., 1971) have documented positive effects on social and adaptive behaviors while youths were in the program, but the data on outcome have been mixed at best.

Braukman, Kirigin, and Wolf (1976) reported that 28 adolescents treated at the original Achievement Place home committed an average of 3.4 legal offenses per year prior to placement in the home and averaged .9 offenses per year while in treatment. Sixteen control subjects who were in residence in other group homes also averaged 3.4 legal offenses per year prior to treatment but committed an average of 7.3 offenses per year while in treatment. However, there was no difference in the number of offenses committed by Achievement Place and comparison youths in the year following discharge from treatment, although Achievement Place youth were institutionalized at less than half the rate (14%) than the comparison youths (31%).

Kirigin, Braukman, Atwater, and Wolf (1982) conducted a larger evaluation of the Teaching Family Model (TFM) by comparing 13 TFM homes with nine comparison group homes. Although youths in TFM homes had lower rates of offense while in treatment, Kirigin et al. found only an insignificant trend for both boys (57% vs. 73%) and girls (27% vs. 47%) treated in TFM homes to have lower legal offense rates following treatment. Similarly, Weinrott, Jones, and Howard (1982) compared the effectiveness of 26 TFM homes with that of 25 other group homes. They found that there were significant improvements in adjustment for youth in both groups but no advantage in treatment effectiveness for the TFM homes, except in the area of academic achievement. They also noted that only 45% of the youths in both samples completed their treatment programs.

Elder, Plants, Welch, and Feindler (1983) applied the TFM to a population of disturbed, neglected, delinquent, and retarded adolescents in a residential psychiatric setting and found that the frequency of injury incidents and aggressive behaviors decreased during treatment but that hospital recidivism did not decrease significantly.

Gossett, Barnhart, Lewis, and Phillips (1977) conducted a long-term follow-up study of adolescents treated in a private psychiatric hospital. They studied 55 boys and girls who had been hospitalized for an average of 7 months. The majority of the youngsters were diagnosed as having behavior disorders, although approximately 25% had psychotic disorders and some were described as neurotic. They conducted follow-up interviews 26 months to 4 years after discharge and found that 62% of the former patients were rated as having a good adjustment, whereas 38% were rated as having a poor adjustment. They found that the diagnostic severity of the patient's psychopathology, the type of treatment termination (complete vs. incomplete treatment), onset of symptomatology (process vs. reactive), whether or not posthospital psychotherapy was obtained, energy level, and amount of acting-out behavior were all related to level of functioning at discharge, with the magnitude of the correlation in the order described above. No control group was used in this study, the rating of outcome was rather subjective and imprecise, and the authors' statistical analysis is somewhat obscure.

An innovative treatment approach for delinquent males in a correctional facility was assessed by Cavior and Schmidt (1978). Treatment interventions, including behavior modification, group and individual therapy, and reality therapy were individualized according to inmates' needs. In addition, recreational and educational programming and involvement in a token economy were provided for all inmates. Improvement while in the facility was documented on a variety of measures;

however, follow-up assessment failed to demonstrate a significant advantage for the innovative program over a traditional juvenile correctional program in terms of parole performance and recidivism. It is discouraging to note that approximately 58% of dischargees from each program had been incarcerated for 60 days or more during the 3-year follow-up period.

Lewis, Lewis, Shanok, Klatskin, and Osborne (1980) also documented improvement during residential treatment but an absence of progress at follow-up. They assessed 51 children who had been treated with milieu therapy, psychodynamic psychotherapy, and special education and found that only 33% were rated as having a favorable outcome, despite indications of therapeutic progress while in the residential facility. Factors that predicted a favorable outcome at follow-up were younger age at admission, less psychotic symptomatology, and less parental psychopathology. Again, this study is of limited utility because of the absence of a control group and the use of subjective and imprecise assessment instruments.

Spence and Marzillier (1981) implemented a study of social skills training with delinquents in a residential setting that did use random assignment to the treatment group, an attention-placebo control group, and a no-treatment control group. They found in-program changes in specified target behaviors for the experimental group, but not the control groups, which were maintained at a 3-month follow-up. Unfortunately, no significant differences were found between the treatment group and control groups on such variables as self-report of delinquency and legal convictions at discharge or follow-up.

Barton, Alexander, Waldron, Turner, and Warburton (1985) reported better results in their study evaluating the results of a behavioral family therapy program with 30 youths in a state training school and their families. They used an alternate treatment comparison group matched on a number of variables, including severity of offenses, and found that at a 15-month follow-up, 60% of the family therapy group had been charged with subsequent offenses versus 93% of the alternate treatment comparison group.

Another outcome study using a delinquent population was conducted by Glick and Goldstein (1987). They implemented an aggression control training program in a residential facility and found that the treatment group performed better than controls on measures of acting-out, impulsiveness, and social skill. They also found that the treatment group was rated as significantly improved in four of six areas of postrelease community functioning.

Prentice-Dunn et al. (1981) examined the effect of nine client variables on outcome at discharge from a residential and day treatment center for 50 preadolescent, emotionally disturbed children. They found that the child's IQ, age, amount of parental involvement during treatment, and "quality" of the child's living situation prior to admission into treatment were all significant predictors of behavioral improvement. Similarly, race, IQ, and parental involvement during treatment were significant predictors of academic improvement.

Schain, Gardella, and Pon (1982) reported on the adjustment of 36 children 4 years after their admission into a residential care program at a state psychiatric hospital. The average age of the children at the time of admission was 12.8 years, and their average duration of treatment was 19.1 months. Twenty-eight percent of the children were in residential mental institutions at follow-up, whereas 67% were residing in some form of home setting. One former patient was in prison, and one was in a juvenile correctional facility. Forty percent of the sample were still receiving some type of psychotherapeutic care, 61% were enrolled in school, and 22% were working. At the time of hospitalization, 87% of the children had exhibited serious violent outbursts. At the time of follow-up, only 30% were classified as seriously violent. Eighty-eight percent of the children in the original sample who had been diagnosed as psychotic (10) were in residential mental health institutions at the time of follow-up, whereas only 11% of the nonpsychotic former patients were in such care.

Blotcky, Dimperio, and Gossett (1984) reviewed 24 long-term (6 months to 24 years) follow-up studies of children under the age of 12 treated in psychiatric hospitals and concluded that good prognosis was positively correlated with "adequate" intelligence, nonpsychotic and nonorganic diagnoses, absence of bizarre symptoms and antisocial features, healthy family functioning, "adequate" length of stay, and involvement in aftercare. They noted a number of methodological flaws in the studies they reviewed and relied upon subjective impressions in determining which trends they felt were valid, but their conclusions are still significant because of the overall consistency of the results obtained by different researchers. It is worth noting that overall, slightly more than 50% of the children with neurotic or personality disorders in the studies reviewed by Blotcky et al. (1984) were reported to have positive long-term outcomes, whereas significantly less than 50% of the children with psychotic disorders, neurological impairment, or below-average intelligence were reported as doing well at follow-up.

Pfeiffer (1989) also found major methodological and conceptual flaws in the majority of the 32 outcome studies of children and adolescents treated in psychiatric facilities that he reviewed. He suggested that future researchers needed to be more careful in defining outcome criteria, needed to develop more ecologically valid measures of treatment and outcome, and needed to use more sophisticated research designs and statistical analyses. Pfeiffer and Strzelecki (1990) later reviewed 34 outcome studies of child and adolescent psychiatric hospitalization from 1975 to 1989. Because only two of the 34 studies reported the means and standard deviations of outcome measures that were necessary to perform statistical aggregation across studies, the authors used a "weighted predictive value" technique that they developed to accomplish such aggregation. They then looked at the ability of 10 variables (nine of which were identical to those used by Blotcky et al., 1984) to predict outcome. They found that the implementation of specific treatment interventions and the provision of aftercare services were the most powerful predictors of positive outcome. Next were the absence of organicity; the absence of bizarre, antisocial, and "primitive" symptoms; diagnosis other than psychosis or aggressive conduct disorder; and high level of family functioning. Length of treatment and intelligence had marginal predictive value, and sex and age at admission were poor predictors of outcome. Overall, the authors concluded that "psychiatric hospitalization of children and adolescents is often beneficial—particularly if a specialized treatment program and aftercare services are available, and if the patient presents with a less pathological clinical picture" (p. 852).

Brendtro and Wasmond (1989) provide a brief review of outcome studies of positive peer-culture treatment programs in residential settings, which concludes that such programs "can have a positive impact on individual youth in areas of self-esteem, personal responsibility, academic achievement, and prosocial values" (p. 94). Unfortunately, the studies that they review provide little follow-up data, relying mostly on in-program psychometric changes as evidence of improvement. A similar review of wilderness programs (Bacon & Kimball, 1989) documents a number of therapeutic changes in youths following enrollment in such programs, including significant reduction in recidivism rates of adjudicated youth (Kelly, 1974; Kelly & Baer, 1968; Willman & Chun, 1973).

Basta and Davidson (1988) conducted a comprehensive review of treatment outcome studies of juvenile offenders from 1980 to 1987, including a number of studies that assessed institutional or community-based residential treatment programs. They did not conduct a separate analysis of residential programs, but they noted that most studies (78%) reported at least one positive treatment effect, even though only 43% of the studies had positive results on recidivism measures. They noted that there were significant methodological flaws in many of the studies but were encouraged that 46% of the studies reviewed employed randomized designs, 67% used multiple measures of behavior, and 54% assessed recidivism at follow-up intervals of 6 months or longer.

Two other reviews of treatment outcome of juvenile offenders have used the technique of meta-analysis (Wolf, 1986) to reanalyze the results found in a number of outcome studies and produce a common measure summarizing these results. Garrett (1985) included only studies assessing treatment programs located in institutional or community residential (e.g., group home) settings. She reviewed 111 studies involving 13,055 subjects from 1960 to 1983. She generally found that behavioral treatment approaches were more effective than psychodynamic or "life skills" approaches and that contingency management, family treatment, and cognitive-behavioral interventions were the most effective specific treatments. Overall, effect sizes were in the modest range, although a discouraging note is the fact that they were significantly lower in studies with more rigorous control procedures than in those with less rigorous controls. Also discouraging is the finding that the outcome measure of recidivism had a much smaller effect size (.13) than other, less ecologically valid measures, such as institutional adjustment (.41) and psychological adjustment (.52).

Whitehead and Lab (1989) also conducted a meta-analysis of juvenile correctional treatment. They included 50 outcome studies published from 1975 to 1984 in their analysis, excluding many others for reasons such as lack of adequate data, absence of a control group, and lack of clear specification of a treatment method. In their analysis, Whitehead and Lab included seven studies that they classified as institutional/residential. Of these seven studies, four yielded negative phi coefficients, indicating an adverse effect of the treatment on the subjects. Of the remaining three studies, only one (Adams & Vetter, 1982) had a statistically significant positive treatment effect. The authors conclude that this analysis provides "little encouragement" regarding the efficacy of residential and institutional interventions for delinquent youth.

The broad-based meta-analytic studies of child treatment outcome that have been done in recent years have largely ignored residential and inpatient treatment as a specific variable. Casey and Berman (1985) reviewed 64 studies assessing outcome of child treatment and reported an overall effect size of .71, indicating that the average treated child was at the 76th percentile of the control group. Their sample included only 8% inpatients, but they did compute an effect size for the inpatient treatment group (.42) that was dramatically lower than the effect size for the outpatient group (1.11). However, this difference may reflect differences in severity of disorder, duration of treatment, or other confounding variables rather than truly representing a difference in the efficacy of inpatient and outpatient treatment. Weisz, Weiss, Alicke, and Klotz (1987) conducted another meta-analysis of child mental health treatment that yielded comparable results (mean effect size = .79) to Casey and Berman's (1985) study, but they specifically excluded interventions involving "relocation to a new living environment." Kazdin, Bass, Ayers, and Rodgers (1990) conducted a meta-analysis of 105 child and adolescent treatment studies that included 3% inpatients and 1% incarcerated adolescents. They reported an overall effect size of .88 compared to no treatment (.77 compared to active control) but did not specifically analyze for inpatient treatment effect. Durlak, Fuhrman, and Lampman (1991) conducted a meta-analysis of 64 treatment studies of preadolescents in which 19% of the subjects were in residential treatment settings. They did not specifically analyze for a residential treatment effect but reported an overall effect size of .56, meaning that the average treated youngster was at the 71st percentile of the untreated group. Weisz, Weiss, Morton, Granger, and Han (1992) conducted a meta-analysis of 110 studies that yielded similar results to the other meta-analyses (mean effect size = .71), but residential or inpatient treatment was not included as a classification variable. Finally, Hazelrigg, Cooper, and Borduin (1987) conducted a meta-analysis of 20 family therapy outcome studies that included three studies involving inpatient treatment (for adolescents or adults). They reported a mean effect size of .45.

SUMMARY

There are several methodological issues that are critical in evaluating the effectiveness of residential and inpatient treatment programs. It is important that treatment outcome be objectively defined, socially relevant, and multidimensional, and it should allow for the separation of treatment effects from maturational change. In addition, it is important that outcome be defined in terms of cost (both monetary and psychosocial) of both treatment and treatment failure. Similarly, it is important that components of treatment programs be specifically and objectively defined so that they can be replicated accurately. It is also important that actual treatment implementation be documented rather than just assumed. Adequacy of research design is another important consideration in the evaluation of residential and inpatient programs. Only in recent years have more adequate research designs yielding clearly interpretable results been found in this area. Another set of important variables that requires adequate definition and specification is child and family characteristics. There has been inadequate research focusing on the interaction between these variables and treatment outcome.

A review of the residential and inpatient evaluation literature suggests that many early studies cited positive results of such treatment, but that these results were actually uninterpretable because of design flaws such as an absence of comparison groups and the use of poorly defined, subjective outcome measures. More recent research generally has indicated that behavioral approaches to residential and inpatient treatment are more effective than are approaches that emphasize intrapsychic interventions. Long-term outcome data are also less encouraging than short-term results. Several child and family characteristics, including higher intelligence, more parental involvement in treatment, and absence of psychotic or delinquent behaviors appear to be related to positive treatment outcome. It is apparent that more research in this area is needed, with more analysis of the effect of specific treatment components and child and family characteristics on specific outcome measures.

5

ALTERNATIVES TO RESIDENTIAL OR INPATIENT TREATMENT

Residential and inpatient treatment for children and adolescents with behavioral and emotional disorders offers unique advantages, primarily maximization of therapeutic impact and control of the treatment environment, but it also entails a number of significant disadvantages—with disruption of a child's and family's life and artificiality of the treatment environment and resulting poor generalization of treatment effects to the home environment among them. In addition, residential and inpatient treatment is extremely expensive (up to $1,000 per day) and is often limited in availability or requires a child to be treated some distance from his or her home. Given these disadvantages, and in light of the less than compelling outcome data for residential and inpatient treatment presented in Chapter 4, it is imperative that both clinicians and mental health systems planners consider alternatives to residential and inpatient treatment. This chapter will present a selected review of the treatment literature concerning alternatives to residential treatment and will discuss guidelines for the appropriate placement of individual cases.

DAY TREATMENT

One of the most attractive alternatives to residential and inpatient treatment for children and adolescents needing mental health care is day treatment or partial hospitalization. As described in Chapter 1, this treatment modality usually involves the child or adolescent client's involvement for 2 to 8 hours per day in a structured series of educational and therapeutic activities. Common components of such programs are academic classwork, group therapy, individual psychotherapy, therapeutic recreation, and occupational therapy. Quite often, in behaviorally oriented day treatment programs, there is an overriding contingency management program in place. Frequently, educational programming is designed to mesh with "regular" school requirements so that children and adolescents enrolled in the day treatment program do not miss out on credits and lose the opportunity for promotion. Another frequently used model is the provision of day treatment services after the regular school day, sometimes with expanded hours of service during the summer school vacation. Under this model, children and adolescents attend the day treatment program for 2 or 3 hours per day, arriving after school is over and leaving in the late afternoon or early evening.

The clear advantages of the day treatment model over outpatient treatment are the opportunity it provides for several hours per day of therapeutic involvement (versus 1 hour per week in traditional outpatient psychotherapy) and the amount of control that clinicians have over the treatment environment. These advantages are particularly important in the implementation of behavioral treatment. Interventions such as time-out and seclusion can be implemented much more easily with trained staff in a controlled day treatment environment than by emotionally involved parents with other demands on their attention at home or by overloaded teachers in a public school who do not have the training, the time, or the appropriate physical facilities to implement such an intervention. Similarly, initial behavioral assessment, which is the foundation of effective behavior therapy and which relies heavily on observational data, can be accomplished more effectively through the direct observations of trained, objective personnel rather than the imprecise and often more subjective observations of parents and teachers.

Day treatment also offers considerable advantages over residential and inpatient care. It is much more conducive to generalization of treatment effects because the child spends one half to three fourths of each day in his or her natural environment. If problems in generalization of treatment effects occur, they can be detected and remediated much earlier than would be possible with residential care, where this difficulty usually is not detected until discharge. Children's roles in their families and communities are not as disrupted as they are by out-of-home care, and parents do not feel as excluded by the treatment process as they often do when their child is in residential or inpatient care. As a result of their greater inclusion in the treatment program, parents often are more willing to learn or implement treatment techniques at home or change circumstances in the home environment that may be maintaining problem behaviors. They also may be more willing to reenter treatment at a later date if problem behaviors recur. Children in more "school-like" day treatment programs often are more invested in their own treatment than are children treated in hospital settings because of the emphasis on individual responsibility inherent in the school environment versus the transfer of responsibility and control to health practitioners in the hospital environment. Similarly, children in day treatment usually feel less stigmatized by their placement than do children in residential or inpatient care. Staff in day treatment programs typically are more educationally and behaviorally oriented than are staff in inpatient settings and thus are more likely to accept behavioral causal explanations and rely on behavioral interventions. Typically, they also have more contact with the child's caretakers and home environment and thus are better able to assess the effects of home variables on the child's behavior than are inpatient or residential staff. The interactive nature of day treatment also creates an environment more conducive to staff outreach efforts, and the similarity to a "normal" school environment allows parents to feel more comfortable and willing to interact with treatment staff.

Although it appears that day treatment offers significant advantages over both outpatient treatment and residential or inpatient treatment, there are significant questions that must be answered concerning the appropriateness of this treatment format for children and adolescents with serious mental health conditions. The first of these questions concerns the effectiveness of day treatment for children with severe conduct or emotional disorders. Does day treatment provide an intense enough treatment environment to effect meaningful change? A secondary question is whether day treatment is safe. Opponents of the use of this treatment modality with seriously disturbed children and adolescents argue that such children cannot be maintained safely in the community during treatment and that failure to place them in the "secure" environment of a hospital ward or residential treatment center will result in danger to themselves or others or the potential for significant property destruction. A brief review of the day treatment outcome literature, with a particular emphasis on studies that compare day treatment to residential or inpatient care, may provide at least partial answers to these questions.

Goldfarb, Goldfarb, and Pollack (1966) matched schizophrenic children on a number of variables, including those reflecting severity of disorder, and then assigned one member of each pair to day treatment and the other to residential treatment. The children's intellectual, academic, and psychiatric status was then assessed over a 3-year treatment period. Children who were less impaired at the beginning of treatment and those whose mental health disorder was thought to be organic in nature showed equivalent improvement in the two treatment settings, whereas those for whom functional causal elements were thought to be dominant improved more in residential care. The most impaired children showed little progress in either setting. Both treatment settings in this study were psychodynamic in orientation, there was no comparison with a no-treatment control group, and there was a great deal of subjectivity in assessment and group assignment. The results only weakly support the idea that residential treatment has a greater impact on children with serious mental illness.

Prentice-Dunn et al. (1981) investigated the treatment outcome of children placed in behaviorally oriented day and residential treatment programs. They found that both groups improved equivalently on behavioral ratings and academic measures, and greater parental involvement was a predictor of improvement in both settings. The two groups were equivalent in severity of disorder, with placement in day treatment rather than residential treatment occurring as a result of family residence within commuting distance to the center.

Velasquez and Lyle (1985) compared the effects of a day treatment program emphasizing counseling and school advocacy to residential treatment for adjudicated youths and status offenders through the use of a quasi-experimental posttest comparison design. They found that, following treatment, both groups showed a significant reduction in status offenses and that there were no significant differences between the groups in school attendance, social workers' assessment of adjustment, or maintenance of a family living situation.

Gabel, Finn, and Ahmad (1988) evaluated the posttreatment placement recommendations for 52 children discharged from a psychiatric day treatment program and found that more than 90% of the children without histories of abuse or neglect, parental substance abuse, suicide behavior/ideation, or severe aggressive behavior were recommended for home placement. In contrast, 100% of the children with histories of three or more of the above factors were recommended for residential care. These findings suggest a differential level of severity of disorder in children appropriate for day treatment and those appropriate for residential care.

Later studies by Gabel and associates, however, have yielded equivocal findings on the issue of differential severity of disorder in children appropriately referred for residential versus day treatment. Gabel and Shindledecker (1990) found that suspected child abuse or parental substance abuse were the determining factors in a referral to out-of-home care rather than the characteristics of the child's own behavior disorder. Gabel and Shindledecker (1992), however, reported that aggressive behavior in adolescents predicted recommendations for out-of-home placement. Gabel, Stadler, and Bjorn (1995) found no clear pattern of greater or lesser psychopathology in boys treated in a day hospital setting versus boys treated in a short-term residential diagnostic setting, although the boys in the day treatment program were significantly younger than the residential boys. They also found that the boys in residential treatment were more likely to be referred for long-term residential care despite the overall equivalence in level of psychopathology between the two groups. It is unclear whether this finding represents a difference in available services, a subtle difference in psychopathology not reflected in psychometric evaluation and behavior ratings, or a greater willingness to recommend children for out-of-home care once they have been removed from home, even for short-term residential treatment.

Grizenko and Papineau (1992) compared the outcome and cost of treating 23 children in a residential treatment unit in a psychiatric hospital with the outcome and cost of treating 23 children in the same unit after it had been converted to a day treatment program. The two groups were not significantly different on a number of variables, including age, diagnosis, severity of psychopathology, and family functioning and support. Results indicated that treatment outcome for the two programs was not significantly different, although there was a trend for better outcome for the day treatment group. Average length of treatment in the day treatment program was 6.1 months versus 19.6 months in the inpatient program, and the average cost per child of treatment for the day treatment program was less than one sixth ($9,213) that of the inpatient program ($61,412). The authors concluded that day treatment is a treatment-effective and cost-effective alternative to residential hospital treatment.

Erker, Searight, Amanat, and White (1993) conducted a long-term follow-up study of adults and adolescents who had received either day ($n = 45$) or residential ($n = 16$) treatment as children. Both groups were in treatment for an average of just over 16 months. There were no significant differences at the time of treatment in severity of disorder, diagnosis, indications of organic involvement, or social and personal adjustment. Ten years after the conclusion of treatment, 66% of the total sample was found to have made positive changes in adjustment, with no significant difference between those who had received day treatment versus those who had received residential treatment. The authors did note that the parents of children in day treatment were significantly more involved in therapy than were the parents of the children in residential treatment and conjectured that this may have been the source of the equivalence in treatment effects. As noted elsewhere in this chapter, the difference in parental involvement may be an integral advantage to the day treatment model.

Carlson, Barr, and Young (1994) examined factors associated with treatment outcome of male juvenile offenders treated in day and residential treatment and found no significant difference in outcome between the two groups. Overall, more than one third of subjects failed to complete treatment, and although 76% of parents felt that their children had shown behavioral improvement, only 35% of the youngsters demonstrated a significant reduction in antisocial behavior. This study did not provide comparison with a control group, and the outcome measures were subjective ratings.

Lyman, Prentice-Dunn, and Wilson (1995) compared children in residential treatment with children in day treatment at the same facility and found that they were rated as having mental health disorders of comparable severity at initiation of treatment. Children in residential treatment were rated by staff, but not by parents, as making significantly greater behavioral improvement during treatment than were children in day treatment. The authors found no significant differences between children in residential and day treatment in academic progress or in the number of disruptive and/or dangerous behavioral incidents occurring during the course of treatment. This last finding is relevant to the argument that children with severe behavioral disorders need to be in residential care to protect themselves and others and suggests that such children can be treated as safely in a non-residential setting as in residential care.

COMMUNITY-BASED TREATMENT

Palmer (1974) examined whether or not delinquent adolescents who were assessed as needing residential treatment prior to community-based treatment actually did better when they received the residential services in addition to the community-based services. Adolescents who were judged as needing such residential services were assigned randomly to either a group that received residential treatment followed by community-based treatment or a group that received community-based treatment immediately. Adolescents who were not judged to require residential care also were assigned randomly to the above groups. Residential treatment was intensive and consisted of individual and group counseling, academic programming, and cultural and recreational activities. The community-based program emphasized counseling and traditional probation and supervision.

The results indicated that the group that was judged to require residential care but did not receive it prior to community-based services had a significantly higher rate of rearrest (94%) during the first 18 months on parole than did the group that was thought to need residential services and did receive them prior to community-based services (58%). The mean number of offenses per month for these two groups were .140 and .066, respectively. Interestingly, for the youths who were not thought to require residential treatment, the number of offenses per month was significantly lower for the group placed directly in community-based services (.067) than for the group that first received unnecessary residential treatment (.107). These results suggest the importance of properly assessing the need for residential treatment in youth and indicate that inappropriate treatment, either in the provision of unnecessary residential care or in the failure to provide such treatment when it is necessary, can have negative consequences.

Winsberg, Bialer, Kupietz, Botti, and Balka (1980) compared the therapeutic outcomes of 49 children randomly assigned to either inpatient care or community-based treatment. A flaw in their experimental design is the fact that all children in both groups were briefly admitted to inpatient care prior to assignment to treatment groups. The children were from 5 to 13 years of age and had received a variety of diagnoses, mainly of externalizing disorders. No children with psychotic disorders were included in the study. The inpatient program emphasized psychotherapy, milieu treatment, and pharmacotherapy, whereas the community-based program consisted of social services and pharmacotherapy without any formal psychotherapy. Both treatment programs averaged 6 months in duration.

Following the 6-month treatment period, outcomes were assessed, and it was found that children in the community-based program showed significantly greater improvement than did the hospital group on behavioral ratings. The hospital group was also rated as less disturbed initially by hospital personnel. Long-term follow-up (1.5 to 3 years later) indicated that almost half of the hospital group later entered residential care, whereas less than 30% of the community-based group required such care. Although the results of this study suggest that community support services may be more efficacious than inpatient care, the two treatment groups do not appear to have been equivalently disturbed at initiation of treatment, and the initial brief hospitalization of both groups makes it difficult to interpret the findings.

One model of community-based intervention that has been replicated and evaluated widely is the Homebuilders model (Kinney et al., 1977). This model consists of intensive, in-home crisis intervention by trained family therapists with families for whom there is a strong possibility that one or more members may have to be removed to an alternative living situation. Common presenting problems for the program include runaway, truancy and school disruption, child abuse, and parental and child substance abuse. Therapists working within the Homebuilders model are on call 24 hours per day and provide case management, behavior modification, crisis intervention, parent training, and family therapy. They often meet with client families in the clients' homes and frequently provide 10 or more hours per week of direct services. The model is intended to provide services only for a month or two during a period of family crisis. When the family has stabilized, more traditional service modalities are substituted for the Homebuilders services. The initial report on the Homebuilders program (Kinney et al., 1977) found that the program was successful in preventing the outside placement of 90% of family members. The authors calculated that this resulted in a monetary savings of $2,300 per client, compared to the projected cost of out-of-home placement. Follow-up, covering 16 months of program operation, indicated that 97% of the clients who avoided out-of-home placement at the time of service delivery were still residing in their homes. Homebuilders appears to be a treatment-effective and cost-effective model, although it requires unusually committed and flexible staff who are permitted to maintain low caseloads in order to provide the intensive treatment that the model specifies.

A follow-up study of the Homebuilders model was conducted by Haapala and Kinney (1988). In this study, 678 status-offending youths who were at imminent risk for removal from their homes were provided with Homebuilders services. During a 12-month follow-up period after the provision of these services, 87% of the youths avoided out-of-home placement. It is worth noting that 34% of the youths had experienced out-of-home care at some point prior to the implementation of the Homebuilders program. Although these results are encouraging, again it should be noted that there is no comparison group and that the youths received traditional counseling services after their termination from Homebuilders, raising the possibility that some of this effect is attributable to those services.

Bath, Richey, and Haapala (1992) conducted another evaluation of Homebuilders model services and found that 83% of 1,506 children served over a 32-month period were not in official out-of-home placement when assessed 12 months after service intake. The authors found that child age was a significant predictor of out-of-home placement, with 0- to 2-year-olds and children 10 years of age and older at greater risk for such placement. Other variables that appeared to predict out-of-home placement were parent mental health problems, single adult caretakers, and receiving public support for the 0- to 2-year-old group; child neglect, child developmental disability, child mental health problems, child special education status, and a child history of in-patient care for the 3- to 9-year-old group; and low family income, delinquency, poor school adjustment, physical violence, runaway, and a history of out-of-home care for the 10- to 17-year-old group. Boys were also significantly more likely than girls to experience out-of-home placement in the 10- to 17-year-old group. These results corroborate the positive results of earlier evaluations of the Homebuilders model but also suggest that the model is not equally applicable to all youths needing services. It appears that a significant number of youngsters receiving Homebuilders services will still require out-of-home care at some point.

Pecora, Fraser, and Haapala (1992) also reported an evaluation of Homebuilders model services with 581 children judged to be at high risk for removal from their homes. They found that the out-of home placement prevention rate at case termination was more than 90% at both of their study sites. The authors of this study also cite two other reports (Feldman, 1990; Yuan et al., 1990) that they say demonstrate that family preservation services such as Homebuilders were correlated not only with high rates of placement prevention but also with significant improvement in child and family functioning.

Bath and Haapala (1993) reported on the application of Homebuilders services to 854 children referred because of abuse or neglect and found that, overall, 13.9% of the children had been removed from their homes at follow-up 12 months after initiation of the Homebuilders intervention. This figure appears to be comparable to outcome data obtained in other evaluations of the Homebuilders model. Interestingly, children who were the victims only of abuse had the lowest placement rate (9.6%), whereas children who were victims of neglect only (15.3%) and of both neglect and abuse (24.2%) had higher rates of placement. The authors reported that the groups experiencing neglect only and both abuse and neglect were quite similar to each other and differed from the abuse-only group on a number of variables. The neglect-only and abuse/neglect families were more reliant on public support and poorer than the abuse-only families. The parents in the neglect-only and abuse/neglect families were also more likely to have mental health, medical, and drug problems and were younger and more often single parents. Again, although these results concerning the effectiveness of intensive in-home family preservation services are encouraging, they are difficult to interpret in the absence of a comparison group.

An emerging model for the provision of mental health treatment and social services to children and adolescents is the "wrap-around" model (VanDenBerg, 1993). This model, rather than basing treatment for all children on one service modality, such as in-home intervention or residential treatment, emphasizes the development of a continuum of treatment services that can be applied individually to a case as needed. In essence, the wrap-around model moves beyond the discussion over residential versus nonresidential treatment to a consideration of which services an individual child or adolescent might require at any point in time.

One of the more ambitious attempts to provide wrap-around services has occurred in North Carolina. There, the Willie M. Program has provided an array of treatment services for seriously emotionally, neurologically, or mentally handicapped youth who are violent or assaultive. These services range from inpatient and residential care to vocational training, structured recreation, and family and individual psychotherapy. Weisz, Walter, Weiss, Fernandez, and Mikow (1990) evaluated the effectiveness of the Willie M. Program. They were prevented by legal constraints from withholding services from a control group, so they compared the effects of long-term involvement in the Willie M. Program (an average of 896 days) with the effects of short-term involvement (an average of 26 days) in the program. One limitation of this study was its reliance on a single outcome measure: arrest rates after termination from the program. Results of the study indicated a somewhat higher arrest rate for the short-term group than for the long-term group, although this difference did not reach statistical significance.

SUMMARY

Residential and inpatient treatment should be considered or evaluated only within the context of a comprehensive continuum of treatment alternatives. One of these alternatives is day treatment, in which children or adolescents attend a therapeutic program for several hours per day but continue to live at home. Day treatment offers more therapeutic contact than does outpatient treatment but does not disrupt a child's life to the same extent as residential or inpatient treatment. The research literature also indicates that day treatment can be an effective treatment approach even for children with severe behavioral and emotional disorders who previously had been thought to require out-of-home treatment.

Community-based treatment is another alternative to residential or inpatient treatment. This modality commonly consists of a variety of counseling, crisis intervention, and case management services delivered to a child and his or her family in their own home or community. Such services generally have been found to be as effective as residential or inpatient treatment at a far lower cost and with less disruption to a child's life and position in the family. It is critical, however, that assessment procedures and prediction models be developed that will allow an accurate determination of which children are best served through which treatment settings and modalities.

Overall, it is hoped that the discussion of residential and inpatient treatment approaches in this book has communicated accurately the complexity and heterogeneity of the field. There are a number of theoretical models of treatment, each with its own set of specific interventions and outcome variables. In addition, nontheoretical variables, such as staffing patterns or the characteristics of children in treatment, vary widely among programs and have considerable impact on treatment procedures and effectiveness. As a result, it is difficult to define prototypical treatment in residential or inpatient settings or to offer simple conclusions regarding its effectiveness or limitations. Clearly, more research is needed to allow us to move beyond a focus on simple main effects and instead look at interactions between client and family characteristics, program characteristics, and outcome. In addition, increasing philosophical and financial pressures are forcing us to evaluate residential and inpatient treatment in comparison to other, less invasive treatment approaches such as day treatment and community-based interventions. Such approaches may offer less behavioral control and environmental insulation than residential and inpatient treatment, but they also involve lower monetary expenditures, less disruption to a child's home life, less worry about inadequate generalization of treatment effects, and less concern about stigma and institutionalization. Future research must address these concerns and provide adequate information to allow clinicians and public planners to make individual and systems decisions that will best meet the treatment needs of all children and adolescents with emotional and behavioral disorders. It appears that residential and inpatient treatment approaches can produce significant benefits but that there is also the risk of significant costs. It is only through continued research and analysis that these benefits and costs can be weighed accurately.

APPENDIX:
RESOURCES ON INPATIENT AND RESIDENTIAL TREATMENT OF CHILDREN AND ADOLESCENTS

This appendix is intended as a resource primarily for mental health professionals and administrators new to the field of inpatient and residential treatment of children and adolescents. Much of the material also will be useful to the parents and families of children and adolescents seeking or already involved in treatment.

SPECIFIC INPATIENT
AND RESIDENTIAL TREATMENT CENTERS

1. Information about inpatient and residential treatment facilities in each state may be obtained by contacting the office of the Commissioner of Mental Health for the state. Local providers of mental health services (e.g., mental health centers, psychiatric clinics) are also good sources of information about local resources.

2. Several organizations of inpatient and residential treatment centers publish directories of their membership (addresses below). These include a directory listing by state of the approximately 350 member agencies of the American Association of Children's Residential Centers (AACRC) ($20) and the approximately 85 organizations meeting national accreditation standards comprising the National Association of Psychiatric Treatment Centers for Children (NAPTCC) ($7.50).

3. Specific programs are discussed in many books and articles in the professional literature. A quick way to identify these is through a computer database such as PsycINFO, which is available in many academic and other libraries.

101

PROFESSIONAL ORGANIZATIONS

Mental health professionals and administrators benefit from the ready access to information, consultation, and other services afforded by affiliating with other professionals in the field. Following are some of the national professional organizations relevant to inpatient and residential treatment of children and adolescents. Other organizations may be identified in Fischer and Schwartz's (1995) *Encyclopedia of Associations,* from which most of the following information was obtained. These include relevant organizations in specific mental health professions. The American Psychological Association, for example, has divisions of Family Psychology; of Child, Youth, and Family Services (and Child Maltreatment Section); and of Clinical Psychology (and Clinical Child Subdivision).

American Association of Children's Residential Centers (AACRC)
1021 Prince St.
Alexandria, VA 22314-2971
PH: (703) 838-7522
FX: (703) 684-5968

American Association of Psychiatric Services for Children (AAPSC)
1200-C Scottsville Rd., Ste. 225
Rochester, NY 14624
PH: (716) 235-6910
TF: (800) 777-6910
FX: (716) 235-0654

National Association of Psychiatric Treatment Centers for Children (NAPTCC)
2000 L St., Ste. 200
Washington, DC 20036
PH: (202) 955-3828
FX: (202) 362-5145

National Association of Children's Hospitals and Related Institutions (NACHRI)
401 Wythe Street
Alexandria, VA 22314
PH: (703) 684-1355
FX: (703) 684-1589

National Association of Homes and Services for Children (NAHSC)
1701 K St. NW, Ste. 200
Washington, DC 20006
PH: (202) 223-3447
FX: (202) 331-7476

LEGAL AND ETHICAL RIGHTS
OF CHILDREN AND ADOLESCENTS

A recently published three-volume set, *Legal Rights of Children* (Kramer, 1994), includes several sections pertinent to work with youngsters in inpatient and residential settings. In particular, sections on "The State's Role in Educating Children," "The State's Role in Caring for and Rearing Children" (especially the chapter on "Children in Institutional Care"), and "Adolescents and Their Legal Rights" are helpful. Kramer reviews laws and court decisions as well as summarizes relevant national standards of care and treatment. Topics in "Children in Institutional Care" include definitions of various institutions, preinstitutionalization due process rights, the least restrictive alternative principle, and children's rights within institutions.

Mental health professionals and educators involved in the educational planning and programming for child and adolescent inpatients and residents should also find Jacob and Hartshorne's (1991) *Ethics and Law for School Psychologists* informative. It discusses particulars of the school psychologist's role in the context of relevant constitutional principles, statutes, case law, and professional ethics of the American Psychological Association. Although intended for a psychological audience, much of the material is relevant and accessible to other professionals involved in education. Koocher and Keith-Spiegel's (1990) *Children, Ethics, and the Law* addresses ethical and legal issues primarily in the context of outpatient psychological treatment, but much is relevant to inpatient and residential settings as well. A useful appendix provides a glossary of major case law decisions cited in the book.

Summaries of court cases and articles appearing in the legal literature during the past couple of decades (Campbell & Lowe, 1995) suggest the following are currently significant issues relevant specifically to inpatient and residential treatment of children and adolescents: who has responsibility, including financial responsibility, for placing children or adolescents in treatment, especially when education of the youngster is a central concern; whether inpatient or residential placement is warranted in certain cases; whether services rendered in inpatient or residential placements are adequate and constitute the least restrictive placement in certain cases; whether confinement in certain institutions or use of certain practices constitutes cruel and unusual punishment; the involuntary commitment of minors, especially the circumstances under which minors' objections to residential or inpatient placement may be considered; and inadequacies in the continuum of mental health services for children and adolescents. The interested reader should consult the resources of a law library.

Some professional organizations publish ethical and professional standards governing the work of members of the organization. The American Psychological Association, for example, publishes the APA Ethical Principles of Psychologists and Code of Conduct and Standards for Educational and Psychological Testing. Organizations may be contacted directly for information.

JOURNALS

The following journals often feature articles relevant to working with seriously emotionally disturbed children or adolescents in residential or inpatient treatment. Most journals with a much broader focus, such as the *American Journal of Psychiatry,* have been omitted. Also excluded from this list are publications devoted to very specific populations, such as the *Journal of Autism and Developmental Disorders,* and those devoted to very specific treatment approaches, such as the *Journal of Strategic and Systemic Therapies* and the *Journal of Applied Behavioral Analysis.*

Adolescence

Adoption and Fostering

American Journal of Orthopsychiatry

Child and Adolescent Psychopharmacology (newsletter)

Child and Adolescent Social Work Journal

Child and Youth Care Forum

Child and Youth Care Quarterly

Child and Youth Services

Children and Society

Children and Youth Services Review
Child Neuropsychology
Child Psychiatry and Human Development
Child Welfare
Community Alternatives: International Journal of Family Care
Crime & Delinquency
Educational and Child Psychology
Education and Treatment of Children
Evaluation and Program Planning
Exceptional Children
Hospital and Community Psychiatry
Japanese Journal of Child and Adolescent Psychiatry
Journal of Adolescent Health
Journal of Child and Adolescent Group Therapy
Journal of Child and Family Studies
Journal of Child Care
Journal of Child and Youth Care
Journal of Clinical Child Psychology
Journal of Child Psychology and Psychiatry and Allied Disciplines
Journal of Child Psychotherapy
Journal of Developmental and Behavioral Pediatrics
Journal of Social Service Research
Journal of the American Academy of Child and Adolescent Psychiatry
Journal of Traumatic Stress
Maladjustment and Therapeutic Education
Research on Social Work Practice
Residential Treatment for Children and Youth
Social Casework
Therapeutic Care and Education

THERAPEUTIC BOOKS, WORKBOOKS, GAMES, AND VIDEOS

Many therapists and counselors use structured, interactive materials to engage children and adolescents in therapy. Some sources of such materials are listed below. The list is not intended to be exhaustive, and consumers are urged to review materials carefully to determine their appropriateness.

A.D.D. Warehouse
300 NW 70th Ave., Suite 102
Plantation, FL 33317
PH: (305) 792-8944
TF: (800) 233-9273

Boulden Publishing Feelings Resources for Children in Distress catalog
PO Box 1186
Weaverville, CA 96093
TF: (800) 238-8433
FX: (916) 623-5525

Childswork/Childsplay
The Center for Applied Psychology
PO Box 61586
King of Prussia, PA 19406
PH: (610) 277-4177
TF: (800) 962-1141
FX: (610) 277-4556

Educational Achievement Systems
319 Nickerson St., Suite 112
Seattle, WA 98109
PH or FX: (206) 820-6111

Faber/Mazlich Workshops, LLC
Dept. 258
PO Box 37
Rye, NY 10580

Feelings Factory
3048 Medlin Drive
Raleigh, NC 27606
PH: (919) 787-8788
TF: (800) 858-2264
FX: (919) 787-1441

Hazelden
15251 Pleasant Valley Rd.
PO Box 176
Center City, MN 55012-0176
TF: (800) 328-9000
FX: (612) 257-1331

HRM Video
Same-Day Service Dept.
175 Tompkins Ave.
Pleasantville, NY 10570-9973
PH: (914) 769-7496
TF: (800) 431-2050
FX: (914) 747-1744

Hunter House, Inc., Publishers
PO Box 2914
Alameda, CA 94501
PH: (510) 865-5282

Morning Glory Press
6595 San Haroldo Way
Buena Park, CA 90620-3748
PH: (714) 828-1998
FX: (714) 828-2049

Ned Owens M.Ed., Inc.
Attention Deficit Disorders Materials
629 W. Centerville Rd.
Garland, TX 75041
(214) 278-1387

New Horizons Press
Small Horizons Series
PO Box 669
Far Hills, NJ 07931
TF: (800) 533-7978

Orchard Books
A Grolier Company
95 Madison Ave.
New York, NY 10016
TF: (800) 621-1115
FX: (800) 374-4329

Paperbacks for Educators
Bibliotherapy for Children and other catalogs
426 West Front St.
Washington, MO 63090
PH: (314) 239-1999
TF: (800) 227-2591
FX: (314) 239-4515

Phillip C. Kendall, PhD
Cognitive-behavioral workbooks for impulsive and anxious children
208 Llanfair Rd.
Ardmore, PA 19003
PH: (610) 896-6387

Research Press
Books and Video Programs catalog
Dept. 96
PO Box 9177
Champaign, IL 61826

Spinoza (bear with tapes)
245 E. 6th Street
St. Paul, MN 55101-1940
PH: (612) 227-3717
TF: (800) CUB-BEAR
FX: (612) 227-1034

Sunburst Communications
39 Washington Ave.
PO Box 40
Pleasantville, NY 10570-0040
TF: (800) 431-1934
FX: (914) 769-2109

Teaching Tales
Channing L. Bete Co., Inc.
200 State Rd.
South Deerfield, MA 01373-0200
TF: (800) 628-7733
FX: (800) 499-6464

Toys "R" Us Toy Guide for Differently Abled Kids
PO Box 8501
Nevada, IA 50201-9968

Western Psychological Services (WPS)
Creative Therapy Store catalog
12031 Wilshire Blvd.
Los Angeles, CA 90025-1251
TF: (800) 648-8857
FX: (310) 478-7838

ASSESSMENT MATERIALS

Psychologists, special educators, and other professionals often use standardized testing or other assessment instruments in their evaluations of children and adolescents. Following are some of the companies that publish such materials. Clinicians are encouraged to consult works such as *Tests* (Pro-Ed, 1991) and *Tests in Print* (Buros Institute of Mental Measurements, 1994) to identify possible assessment instruments, references pertinent to the psychometric properties of measures, and information on publishers. Good tests have accompanying technical information about norms, reliability and validity data, and other important information. Many professional books and journals also publish relevant research findings and clinical information.

American Guidance Service
4201 Woodland Rd.
PO Box 99
Circle Pines, MN 55014-1796
TF: (800) 328-2560
FX: (612) 786-9077

Child Behavior Checklist
University Medical Education Associates
1 S. Prospect St.
Burlington, VA 05401-3456
PH: (802) 656-8313
(802) 656-4563
FX: (802) 656-2602

CPPC
4 Conant Sq.
Brandon, VT 05733
PH: (802) 247-6871
TF: (800) 433-8234
FX: (802) 247-6853

Educational Achievement Systems
319 Nickerson, Suite 112
Seattle, WA 98109
PH or FX: (206) 820-6111

Hawthorne Educational Services, Inc.
800 Gray Oak Dr.
Columbia, MO 65201
PH: (314) 874-1710
TF: (800) 542-1673
FX: (800) 442-9509

Jastak Associates
A Division of Wide Range, Inc.
PO Box 3410
Wilmington, DE 19804-0250
PH: (302) 652-4990
TF: (800) 221-WRAT
FX: (302) 652-1644

Mental Health Systems (MHS)
908 Niagara Falls Blvd.
North Tonawanda, NY 14120-2060
TF: (800) 456-3003
FX: (416) 424-1736

Psychological Assessment Resources, Inc. (PAR)
PO Box 998
Odessa, FL 33556
TF: (800) 331-TEST
FX: (800) 727-9329

Pro-Ed
8700 Shoal Creek Blvd.
Austin, TX 78757-6897
TF: (800) 397-7633
FX: (800) FXP-ROED

Psychological Corporation
Harcourt Brace & Co.
555 Academic Ct.
San Antonio, TX 78204-2498
TF: (800) 228-0752
FX: (800) 232-1223

Riverside Publishing Co.
A Houghton Mifflin Co.
8420 Bryn Mawr Ave.
Chicago, IL 60631
TF: (800) 767-8378
FX: (312) 693-0325

Sigma Assessment Systems, Inc.
Research Psychologists Press Division
PO Box 610984
Port Huron, MI 48061-0984
TF: (800) 265-1285
FX: (800) 361-9411

Slosson Educational Publications, Inc.
PO Box 280
East Aurora, NY 14052-0280
TF: (800) 828-4800
FX: (800) 655-3840

Western Psychological Services (WPS)
12031 Wilshire Blvd.
Los Angeles, CA 90025-1251
TF: (800) 648-8857
FX: (310) 478-7838

ADVOCACY, SUPPORT, AND SELF-HELP ORGANIZATIONS

Children and adolescents in treatment, as well as their parents and other family members, including foster families, may benefit from participation in a variety of supportive and educational organizations. Some of these organizations address the clinical or educational needs of the identified patients and provide information to both professionals and consumers. Others help family members cope with the stresses and dysfunction that often affect patients' family systems. Some help the patients and families learn better how to navigate the mental health, social welfare, educational, and legal systems in which they find themselves. Mental health professionals should become familiar with local resources, so they may refer patients and/or their families to the organizations most likely to benefit them.

Following are some of the national organizations that often have state and/or local branches likely to be of interest to many families involved in inpatient or residential treatment. Many other organizations exist that might address concerns peculiar to specific families, including families of various ethnic and cultural backgrounds. Many religious organizations also provide support services and organizations. Consumers are encouraged to inquire about local organizations and to consult Fischer and Schwartz's (1995) *Encyclopedia of Associations,* from which the following information was obtained. Consumers should evaluate any organizations they contact to verify whether the organization indeed offers needed services.

Alcohol and Other Substance Abuse

Adult Children Anonymous (ACA)
Region 8
P.O. Box 150331
Arlington, TX 76015
PH: (817) 478-3191

Al-Anon Family Group Headquarters (AFG)
P.O. Box 862, Midtown Sta.
New York, NY 10018
PH: (212) 302-7240
TF: (800) 356-9996

Alateen
Same address and numbers as Al-Anon
Alcoholics Anonymous World Services (AA)
475 Riverside Drive
New York, NY 10163
PH: (212) 870-3400
FX: (212) 870-3003

Cocaine Anonymous World Services (CAWS)
3740 Overland Ave., Ste. H
Los Angeles, CA 90034-6337
PH: (310) 559-5833
TF: (800) 347-8998

Drug-Anon Focus
PO Box 20806, Park West Station
New York, NY 10025
PH: (212) 484-9095

Families Anonymous (FA)
PO Box 3475
Culver City, CA 90231-3475
PH: (310) 313-5800
TF: (800) 736-9805

"Just Say No" International
2101 Webster Street, Ste. 1300
Oakland, CA 94612
PH: (510) 451-6666
TF: (800) 258-2766

Narcotics Anonymous (NA)
PO Box 9999
Van Nuys, CA 91409
PH: (818) 780-3951

Toughlove International
PO Box 1069
Doylestown, PA 18901
PH: (215) 348-7090
TF: (800) 333-1069
FX: (215) 348-9874

Child Abuse and Molestation

Child Abuse Listening and Mediation (CALM)
PO Box 90754
Santa Barbara, CA 93190-0754
PH: (805) 965-2376

Molesters Anonymous (M.AN)
c/o Batterers Anonymous
8485 Tamarind, Ste. D
Fontana, CA 92335
PH: (909) 355-1100

Parents Anonymous (PA)
675 W. Foothill Blvd., Ste. 220
Claremont, CA 91711-3416
PH: (909) 621-6184
FX: (909) 625-6304

Divorce, Child Custody, and Stepfamilies

Divorced Parents X-Change
PO Box 1127
Athens, OH 45701-1127
PH: (614) 664-2114

Mothers Without Custody (MWOC)
PO Box 27418
Houston, TX 77227-7418
PH: (713) 840-1622
TF: (800) 457-MWOC

Stepfamily Association of America (SAA)
215 Centennial Mall S., Ste. 212
Lincoln, NE 68508
PH: (402) 477-7837
TF: (800) 735-0329
FX: (402) 477-8317

Stepfamily Foundation (SF)
333 West End Ave.
New York, NY 10023
PH: (212) 877-3244
TF: (800) SKY-STEP
FX: (212) 362-7030

Foster Parenting, Adoption, and Reunification

American Foster Care Resources (AFCR)
PO Box 271
King George, VA 22485
PH: (703) 775-7410

Child Welfare Institute (CWI)
1349 W. Peachtree NE, Ste. 900
Atlanta, GA 30309
PH: (404) 876-1934
FX: (404) 876-7949

National Foster Parent Association (NFPA)
Information and Services Office
226 Kilts Dr.
Houston, TX 77024
PH: (713) 467-1850
FX: (713) 827-0919

Orphan Foundation of America (OFA)
1500 Massachusetts Ave., NW, Ste. 448
Washington, DC 20005
PH: (202) 861-0762
(202) 223-6235
TF: (800) 950-4673
FX: (202) 223-9079

Mental Health/Mental Illness

National Alliance for the Mentally Ill (NAMI)
2101 Wilson Blvd., Ste. 302
Arlington, VA 22201
PH: (703) 524-7600
FX: (703) 524-9094

National Mental Health Association (NMHA)
1021 Prince St.
Alexandria, VA 22314-2971
PH: (703) 684-7722
TF: (800) 969-NMHA
FX: (703) 684-5968

Referral to Other Organizations

Mental Illness Foundation
420 Lexington Ave., No. 2104
New York, NY 10170-0002
PH: (212) 629-0755
FX: (212) 629-3117

National Self-Help Clearinghouse (NSHC)
25 W. 43rd St., Rm. 620
New York, NY 10036-7406
PH: (212) 354-8525
FX: (212) 642-1956

Self-Help Center
Div. of MHAI
150 N. Wacker Dr., Ste. 900
Chicago, IL 60606
PH: (312) 368-9070
FX: (312) 368-0283

Relationships

Co-Dependents Anonymous (CoDA)
PO Box 33577
Phoenix, AZ 85067-3577
PH: (602) 277-7991

Love-N-Addiction (LNA)
PO Box 759
Williamantic, CT 06226
PH: (203) 423-2344

Special Education, Including Learning Disabilities

Learning Disabilities Association of America (LDA)
4156 Library Rd.
Pittsburgh, PA 15234
PH: (412) 341-1515
FX: (412) 344-0224

National Center for Learning Disabilities (NCLD)
381 Park Ave., S., Ste. 1420
New York, NY 10016
PH: (212) 545-7510
FX: (212) 545-9665

LEGAL ASSISTANCE FOR
CLIENTS AND THEIR FAMILIES

Children and adolescents who require inpatient or residential treatment, along with their families, often present with important legal as
well as mental health concerns. The following organizations litigate
cases and/or provide assistance to attorneys and others involved in
addressing these legal issues (Fischer & Schwartz, 1995; Kramer,
1994).

American Bar Association Center on Children and the Law (ABACCL)
1800 M St., NW
Washington, DC 20036
PH: (202) 331-2250
FX: (202) 331-2225

American Professional Society on the Abuse of Children
332 S. Michigan Ave., Ste. 1600
Chicago, IL 60604
PH: (312) 554-0166

National Association of Counsel for Children (NACC)
1205 Oneida St.
Denver, CO 80220
PH: (303) 322-2260
FX: (303) 327-3523

National Center on Women and Family Law (NCOWFL)
799 Broadway, Ste. 402
New York, NY 10003
PH: (212) 674-8200
FX: (212) 533-5104

National Center for Youth Law (NCYL)
114 Sansome St., Ste. 900
San Francisco, CA 94104
PH: (415) 543-3307
FX: (415) 956-9024

REFERENCES

Adams, R., & Vetter, H. J. (1982). Social structure and psychodrama outcome: A ten-year follow-up. *Journal of Offender Counseling, Services, and Rehabilitation, 6,* 111-119.

Aichorn, A. (1935). *Wayward youth.* New York: Viking.

Allerhand, M. E., Weber, R., & Haug, M. (1966). *Adaptation and adaptability: The Bellefaire follow-up study.* New York: Child Welfare League.

American Psychiatric Association. (1994). *Diagnostic and statistical manual of mental disorders* (4th ed.). Washington, DC: Author.

Angold, A., & Pickles, A. (1993). Seclusion on an adolescent unit. *Journal of Child Psychology and Psychiatry, 34,* 975-989.

Axline, V. M. (1947). *Play therapy.* Boston: Houghton Mifflin.

Azrin, N. H., Sneed, T. J., & Foxx, R. M. (1974). Dry-bed training: Rapid elimination of childhood enuresis. *Behavior Research and Therapy, 12,* 147-156.

Azrin, N. H., & Wesolowski, M. D. (1974). Theft reversal: An overcorrection procedure for eliminating stealing by retarded persons. *Journal of Applied Behavior Analysis, 7,* 577-581.

Bacon, S. B., & Kimball, R. (1989). The wilderness challenge model. In R. D. Lyman, S. Prentice-Dunn, & S. Gabel (Eds.), *Residential and inpatient treatment of children and adolescents.* New York: Plenum.

Barber, C. C., Colson, D. B., McParland, M. Q., O'Malley, F., Pope, K. K., & Coyne, L. (1994). Child abuse and treatment difficulty in inpatient treatment of children and adolescents. *Child Psychiatry and Human Development, 25,* 53-64.

Barker, P. (1982). Residential treatment for disturbed children: Its place in the '80s. *Canadian Journal of Psychiatry, 27,* 634-639.

Barker, P. (1993). The future of residential treatment for children. In C. E. Schaefer & A. J. Swanson (Eds.), *Children in residential care: Critical issues in treatment* (pp. 1-16). Northvale, NJ: Jason Aronson.

Barton, C., Alexander, J. F., Waldron, H., Turner, C. W., & Warburton, J. (1985). Generalizing treatment effects of functional family therapy: Three replications. *American Journal of Family Therapy, 13,* 16-26.

Basta, J. M., & Davidson, W. S. (1988). Treatment of juvenile offenders: Study outcomes since 1980. *Behavioral Sciences and the Law, 6,* 355-384.

Bath, H. I., & Haapala, D. A. (1993). Intensive family preservation services with abused and neglected children: An examination of group differences. *Child Abuse & Neglect, 17,* 213-225.

Bath, H. I., Richey, C. A., & Haapala, D. A. (1992). Child age and outcome correlates in intensive family preservation services. *Children and Youth Services Review, 14,* 389-406.

Beker, J., & Feuerstein, R. (1990). Conceptual foundations of the Modifying Environment in group care and treatment settings for children and youth. *Journal of Child and Youth Care, 4*(5), 23-33.

Beker, J., & Feuerstein, R. (1991). The Modifying Environment and other environmental perspectives in group care: A conceptual contrast and integration. *Residential Treatment for Children & Youth, 8,* 21-37.

Bereika, G. M., & Mikkelsen, E. J. (1992). Individualized residential treatment as an alternative to acute psychiatric hospitalization for children and adolescents. *Community Alternatives, 4,* 97-117.

Berlin, I. N., & Hendren, R. L. (1991). Effective treatment planning. In R. L. Hendren & I. N. Berlin (Eds.), *Psychiatric care of children and adolescents: A multicultural approach* (pp. 66-87). New York: Wiley.

Beskind, H. (1962). Psychiatric inpatient treatment of adolescents. *Comprehensive Psychiatry, 3,* 354-369.

Bettelheim, B. (1950). *Love is not enough.* New York: Free Press.

Bettelheim, B. (1974). *A home for the heart.* New York: Knopf.

Bettelheim, B., & Sanders, J. (1979). Milieu therapy: the Orthogenic School model. In J. D. Noshpitz (Ed.), *Basic handbook of child psychiatry* (Vol. 3, pp. 216-230). New York: Basic Books.

Blair, D. T. (1991). Assaultive behavior: Does it begin in the front office? *Journal of Psychosocial Nursing, 5,* 21-26.

Blair, D. T., & New, S. A. (1991). Assaultive behavior: Know the risk. *Journal of Psychosocial Nursing, 11,* 25-30.

Blase, K. A., Fixsen, D. L., Freeborn, K., & Jaeger, D. (1989). The behavioral model. In R. D. Lyman, S. Prentice-Dunn, & S. Gabel (Eds.), *Residential and inpatient treatment of children and adolescents* (pp. 43-59). New York: Plenum.

Bleiberg, E. (1989). Stages of residential treatment: Application of a developmental model. *Residential Treatment for Children & Youth, 6,* 7-28.

Blotcky, J. M., Dimperio, T. C., & Gossett, J. T. (1984). Follow-up of children treated in psychiatric hospitals: A review of studies. *American Journal of Psychiatry, 141,* 1499-1507.

Braga, W. de C. (1989). Youth suicide risk assessment: Process and model. *Residential Treatment for Children & Youth, 7,* 1-21.

Braga, W. de C. (1993). Experience with alleged sexual abuse in residential program: II. Problems in the management of allegations. *Residential Treatment for Children & Youth, 11,* 99-116.

Braukmann, C. J., Kirigin, K. A., & Wolf, M. W. (1976, August). *Achievement Place: The researchers perspective.* Paper presented at the annual meeting of the American Psychological Association, Washington, DC.

Brendtro, L. K., & Wasmond, W. (1989). The peer culture model. In R. D. Lyman, S. Prentice-Dunn, & S. Gabel (Eds.), *Residential and inpatient treatment of children and adolescents* (pp. 81-96). New York: Plenum.

Brown, J. S., & Tooke, S. K. (1992). On the seclusion of psychiatric patients. *Social Science Medicine, 35,* 711-721.

Browning, R. M., & Stover, D. O. (1971). *Behavior modification in child treatment.* Chicago: Aldine.

Buehler, R. E., Patterson, G. R., & Furniss, J. M. (1966). The reinforcement of behavior in institutional settings. *Behavior Research and Therapy, 4,* 157-167.

Buros Institute of Mental Measurements. (1994). *Tests in print IV: An index to tests, test reviews, and the literature on specific tests.* Lincoln: University of Nebraska, Buros Institute of Mental Measurements.

Caldwell, B., & Rejino, E. (1993). Ensuring that all children and adolescents in residential treatment live in a protected, safe environment. *Residential Treatment for Children & Youth, 11,* 49-62.

Campbell, N. C., & Lowe, D. (1995). *Computerized literature review, West Law and Lexis data bases.* Tuscaloosa: University of Alabama, Law Center Library.

Carlo, P. (1985). The children's residential treatment center as a living laboratory for family members: A review of the literature and its implications for practice. *Child Care Quarterly, 14,* 156-170.

Carlson, B. E., Barr, W. B., & Young, K. J. (1994). Factors associated with treatment outcomes of male adolescents. In G. Northrup (Ed.), *Applied research in residential treatment* (pp. 39-58). New York: Haworth.

Casey, R. J., & Berman, J. S. (1985). The outcome of psychotherapy with children. *Psychological Bulletin, 98,* 388-400.

Cates, J. A. (1991). Residential treatment in the 1980s: Part I: Characteristics of children served. *Residential Treatment of Children & Youth, 9,* 75-84.

Cavior, H. E., & Schmidt, A. A. (1978). Test of the effectiveness of a differential treatment strategy at the Robert F. Kennedy Center. *Criminal Justice and Behavior, 5,* 131-139.

Charles, G., & Matheson, J. (1991). Suicide prevention and intervention with young people in foster care in Canada. *Child Welfare, 70,* 185-191.

Clark, H. B., Caldwell, C. P., & Christian, W. P. (1979). Classroom training of conversational skills and remote programming for the practice of these skills in another setting. *Child Behavior Therapy, 1,* 139-160.

Coates, R. B., & Miller, A. D. (1972). Neutralization of community resistance to group homes. In Y. Bakal (Ed.), *Closing correctional institutions* (pp. 67-84). Lexington, MA: D. C. Heath.

Cohen, H. L., & Filipczak, J. (1971). *A new learning environment: A case for learning.* San Francisco: Jossey-Bass.

Colyar, D. E. (1991). Residential care and treatment of youths with conduct disorders: Conclusions of a conference of child care workers. *Child & Youth Forum, 20,* 195-204.

Conway, J. B., & Bucher, B. D. (1976). Transfer and maintenance of behavior change in children: A review and suggestions. In J. Mash, L. A. Hamenlynck, & L. C. Handy (Eds.), *Behavior modification and families* (pp. 119-159). New York: Brunner/ Mazel.

Corcoran, K. J. (1993). Understanding and coping with burnout. In C. E. Schaefer & C. J. Swanson (Eds.), *Children in residential care: Critical issues in treatment* (pp. 251-262). Northvale, NJ: Jason Aronson.

Cormack, P. H. (1993a). Quality assurance. In C. E. Schaefer & A. J. Swanson (Eds.), *Children in residential care: Critical issues in treatment* (pp. 191-218). Northvale, NJ: Jason Aronson.

Cormack, P. H. (1993b). Special and unusual events in residential treatment: Theoretical and clinical perspectives. In C. E. Schaefer & A. J. Swanson (Eds.), *Children in residential care: Critical issues in treatment* (pp. 89-103). Northvale, NJ: Jason Aronson.

Cornsweet, C. (1990). A review of research on hospital treatment of children and adolescents. *Bulletin of the Menninger Clinic, 54,* 64-77.

Cotton, N. S. (1989). The developmental-clinical rationale for the use of seclusion in the psychiatric treatment of children. *American Journal of Orthopsychiatry, 59,* 442-450.

Cox, R. D., & Schopler, E. (1991). Social skills training in children. In M. Lewis (Ed.), *Child and adolescent psychiatry: A comprehensive textbook* (pp. 903-908). Baltimore: Williams & Wilkins.

Craft, M., Stephenson, G., & Granger, C. (1964). A controlled trial of authoritarian and self-governing regimens with adolescent psychopaths. *American Journal of Orthopsychiatry, 34,* 543-554.

Crenshaw, D. A. (1993). Responding to sexual acting-out. In C. E. Schaefer & A. J. Swanson (Eds.), *Children in residential care: Critical issues in treatment* (pp. 50-76). Northvale, NJ: Jason Aronson.

Crespi, T. D. (1990). Restraint and seclusion with institutionalized adolescents. *Adolescence, 25,* 825-829.

Curry, J. F. (1991). Outcome research on residential treatment: Implications and suggested directions. *American Journal of Orthopsychiatry, 61,* 348-357.

Dahms, W. R. (1978). Authority vs. relationship? *Child Care Quarterly, 7,* 336-344.

Dalton, R., Bolding, D. D., Woods, J., & Daruna, J. H. (1987). Short-term psychiatric hospitalization of children. *Hospital and Community Psychiatry, 38,* 973-976.

Davids, A., Ryan, R., & Salvatore, P. (1968). Effectiveness of residential treatment. *American Journal of Orthopsychiatry, 38,* 469-475.

Davids, A., & Salvatore, P. (1976). Residential treatment of disturbed children and adequacy of their subsequent adjustment: A follow-up study. *American Journal of Orthopsychiatry, 46,* 63-73.

Diamond, A. (1993). The establishment and maintenance of the director's influence on a residential treatment program. In C. E. Schaefer & A. J. Swanson (Eds.), *Children in residential care: Critical issues in treatment* (pp. 147-159). Northvale, NJ: Jason Aronson.

Dinoff, M., Rickard, H. C., Love, W., & Elder, I. (1978). A patient writes his own report. *Adolescence, 13,* 135-141.

Doyle, J. S., & Bauer, S. K. (1989). Post-traumatic stress disorder in children: Its identification and treatment in a residential setting for emotionally disturbed youth. *Journal of Traumatic Stress, 2,* 275-288.

Drabman, R. S., Spitalnik, R., & O'Leary, K. D. (1973). Teaching self-control to disruptive children. *Journal of Abnormal Psychology, 82,* 10-16.

Duchnowski, A. J., & Friedman, R. M. (1990). Children's mental health: Challenges for the nineties. *Journal of Mental Health Administration, 17,* 3-12.

Durlak, J. A., Fuhrman, T., & Lampman, C. (1991). Effectiveness of cognitive-behavior therapy for maladapting children: A meta-analysis. *Psychological Bulletin, 110,* 204-214.

Durrant, M. (1993). *Residential treatment: A cooperative, competency-based approach to therapy and program design.* New York: Norton.

Elder, J. P., Edelstein, B. A., & Narick, M. M. (1979). Adolescent psychiatric patients: Modifying aggressive behavior with social skills training. *Behavior Modification, 3,* 161-178.

Elder, J. P., Plants, D., Welch, H. J., & Feindler, E. L. (1983). Achievement Place in a psychiatric setting: Program evaluation. *Journal of Psychiatric Treatment and Evaluation, 5,* 337-344.

Emery, R. E., & Marholin, D. (1977). An applied behavior analysis of delinquency: The irrelevancy of relevant behavior. *American Psychologist, 32,* 860-873.

Endres, V. J., & Goke, D. H. (1973). Time-out rooms in residential treatment centers. *Child Welfare, 52,* 359-366.

Erker, G. J., Searight, H. R., Amanat, E., & White, P. D. (1993). Residential versus day treatment for children: A long-term follow-up study. *Child Psychiatry and Human Development, 24,* 31-39.

Everett, C. A., & Volgy, S. S. (1993). Treating the child in systemic family therapy. In T. K. Kratochwil & R. J. Morris (Eds.), *Handbook of psychotherapy with children and adolescents* (pp. 247-257). Boston: Allyn & Bacon.

Famularo, R., Kinscherff, R., & Fenton, T. (1990). Symptom differences in acute and chronic presentation of childhood post-traumatic stress disorder. *Child Abuse & Neglect, 14,* 439-444.

Fassler, D., & Cotton, N. (1992). A national survey on the use of seclusion in the psychiatric treatment of children. *Hospital and Community Psychiatry, 43,* 370-374.

Feldman, L. (1990). *Evaluating the impact of family preservation services in New Jersey.* Trenton, NJ: New Jersey Division of Youth and Family Services; Bureau of Research, Evaluation, and Quality Assurance.

Ferster, C. B. (1961). Positive reinforcement and behavioral deficits of autistic children. *Child Development, 32,* 437-456.

Fischer, C. A., & Schwartz, C. A. (1995). *Encyclopedia of associations: 1996* (30th ed.). New York: Gale Research.

Flackett, J. M., & Flackett, G. (1970). Criswell House: An alternative to institutional treatment for juvenile offenders. *Federal Probation, 34,* 30-37.

Freedman, A. M., Kaplan, H. I., & Sadock, B. J. (1972). Child psychiatry: Introduction. In A. M. Freedman, H. I. Kaplan, & B. J. Sadock (Eds.), *Modern synopsis of comprehensive textbook of psychiatry* (pp. 574-583). Baltimore: Williams & Wilkins.

Freeman, G. W., Spilka, B., & Mason, R. C. (1968, May). *Delinquency and the Outward Bound program: An empirical evaluation of a radical approach to delinquency.* Paper presented at the convention of the Rocky Mountain Psychological Association, Denver.

Friedman, R. M., & Street, S. (1985). Admission and discharge criteria for children's mental health services: A review of the issues and options. *Journal of Clinical Child Psychology, 14,* 229-235.

Gabel, S., Finn, M., & Ahmed, A. (1988). Day treatment outcome with severely disturbed children. *Journal of the American Academy of Child and Adolescent Psychiatry, 176,* 323-331.

Gabel, S., & Shindledecker, R. (1990). Parental substance abuse and child abuse/maltreatment predict poor outcome in children's inpatient treatment. *Journal of the American Academy of Child and Adolescent Psychiatry, 29,* 919-924.

Gabel, S., & Shindledecker, R. (1992). Adolescent psychiatric inpatients: Characteristics, outcome and comparison between discharged patients from specialized and nonspecialized adolescent units. *Journal of Youth and Adolescence, 21,* 1-17.

Gabel, S., Stadler, J., & Bjorn, J. (1995). Behavioral and family characteristics of boys in day hospital and residential settings: Is there a relationship to placement recommendations? *Continuum, 2,* 57-69.

Gadpaille, W. J. (1985). Psychiatric treatment of the adolescent. In H. I. Kaplan & B. J. Sadock (Eds.), *Comprehensive textbook of psychiatry* (4th ed., pp. 1805-1812). Baltimore: Williams & Wilkins.

Galaway, B. (1991). Belonging and permanence: An interview with Dr. Karl Menninger. *Community Alternatives, 3,* 1-8.

Garrett, C. J. (1985). Effects of residential treatment on adjudicated delinquents: A meta-analysis. *Journal of Research in Crime and Delinquency, 22,* 287-308.

Gibson, P. (1981). The effects of and the correlates of success in a wilderness therapy program for problem youths (Doctoral dissertation, Columbia University, 1981). *Dissertation Abstracts International, 42,* 140A.

Gil, E. (1982). Institutional abuse from a family systems perspective: A working paper. *Child & Youth Services: Institutional Abuse of Children & Youth, 4,* 7-13.

Glick, B., & Goldstein, A. P. (1987). Aggression replacement training. *Journal of Counseling and Development, 65,* 356-362.

Goldberg, K. (1991). Family experiences of residential treatment. *Journal of Child and Youth Care, 6,* 1-6.

Goldfarb, W., Goldfarb, N., & Pollack, R. C. (1966). Treatment of childhood schizophrenia: A three year comparison of day and residential treatment. *Archives of General Psychiatry, 14,* 119-128.

Goldstein, A. P., & Glick, B. (1994). Aggression replacement training: Curriculum and evaluation. *Simulation & Gaming, 25,* 9-26.

Goldstein, A. P., Sherman, M., Gershaw, N. J., Sprafkin, R. P., & Glick, B. (1978). Training aggressive adolescents in prosocial behavior. *Journal of Youth and Adolescence, 7,* 73-92.

Goren, S., Abraham, I., & Doyle, N. (in press). Reducing violence in a child psychiatric hospital through planned organizational change. *Journal of Child and Adolescent Psychiatric Nursing.*

Goren, S., & Curtis, W. J. (1995). *Staff beliefs about seclusion and restraint in child psychiatric hospitals.* Unpublished manuscript.

Goren, S., Singh, N. N., & Best, A. M. (1993). The aggression-coercion cycle: Use of seclusion and restraint in a child psychiatric hospital. *Journal of Child and Family Studies, 2,* 61-73.

Gossett, J. T., Barnhart, D., Lewis, J. M., & Phillips, V. A. (1977). Follow-up of adolescents treated in a psychiatric hospital: Predictors of outcome. *Archives of General Psychiatry, 34,* 1037-1042.

Grizenko, N., & Papineau, D. (1992). A comparison of the cost-effectiveness of day treatment and residential treatment for children with severe behavior problems. *Canadian Journal of Psychiatry, 37,* 393-400.

Gwynn, C., Meyer, R., & Schaefer, C. (1993). The influence of peer culture in residential treatment. In C. E. Schaefer & A. J. Swanson (Eds.), *Children in residential care: Critical issues in treatment* (pp. 104-133). Northvale, NJ: Jason Aronson.

Haapala, D. A., & Kinney, J. M. (1988). Avoiding out-of-home placement of high-risk status offenders through the use of intensive home-base family preservation services. *Criminal Justice and Behavior, 15,* 334-348.

Hagen, J. V. (1993). Family work in residential treatment. In C. E. Schaefer & A. J. Swanson (Eds.), *Children in residential care: Critical issues in treatment* (pp. 134-144). Northvale, NJ: Jason Aronson.

Handen, B. L. (1995). Behavior therapy and pharmacological adjuncts. In R. T. Ammerman & M. Hersen (Eds.), *Handbook of child behavior therapy in the psychiatric setting* (pp. 109-132). New York: Wiley.

Harkavy, J., Johnson, S. B., Silverstein, J., Spillar, R., McCallum, M., & Rosenbloom, A. (1983). Who learns what at diabetes summer camp. *Journal of Pediatric Psychology, 8,* 143-153.

Hartmann, E., Glasser, B., Greenblatt, M., Soloman, M., & Levinson, D. (1968). *Adolescents in a mental hospital.* New York: Grune & Stratton.

Hazelrigg, M. D., Cooper, H. M., & Borduin, C. M. (1987). Evaluating the effectiveness of family therapies: An integrative review and analysis. *Psychological Bulletin, 101,* 428-442.

Hendren, R. L. (1991). Determining the need for inpatient treatment. In R. L. Hendren & I. N. Berlin (Eds.), *Psychiatric inpatient care of children and adolescents: A multicultural approach* (pp. 37-65). New York: Wiley.

Herman, S. H., & Tramontana, J. (1971). Instructions and group versus individual reinforcement in modifying disruptive group behavior. *Journal of Applied Behavior Analysis, 4,* 113-120.

Herrera, E. G., Lifsom, B. G., Hartmann, E., & Soloman, M. H. (1974). A 10-year follow-up of 55 hospitalized adolescents. *American Journal of Psychiatry, 31,* 769-774.

Hobbs, N. (1966). Helping disturbed children: Ecological and psychological strategies. *American Psychologist, 21,* 1105-1115.

Irwin, M. (1987). Are seclusion rooms needed on child psychiatric units? *American Journal of Orthopsychiatry, 57*(1), 125-126.

Jacob, S., & Hartshorne, T. S. (1991). *Ethics and law for school psychologists.* Brandon, VT: Clinical Psychology Publishing.

James, L., & Wherry, J. N. (1991). Suicide in residential treatment: Causes, assessment, and treatment issues. *Residential Treatment for Children & Youth, 9,* 23-36.

Jemerin, J. M., & Philips, I. (1988). Changes in inpatient child psychiatry: Consequences and recommendations. *Journal of the American Academy of Child and Adolescent Psychiatry, 27,* 397-403.

Jesness, C. F. (1971). The Preston Typology Study: An experiment with differential treatment in an institution. *Journal of Research in Crime and Delinquency, 8,* 38-52.

Jesness, C. F. (1975). Comparative effectiveness of behavior modification and transactional analysis programs for delinquents. *Journal of Consulting and Clinical Psychology, 43,* 758-779.

Johnson, C. R. (1995). Unit structure and behavioral programming. In R. T. Ammerman & M. Hersen (Eds.), *Handbook of child behavior therapy in the psychiatric setting* (pp. 133-149). New York: Wiley.

Johnson, M. R., Whitman, T. L., & Barloon-Noble, R. (1978). A home-based program for a preschool, behaviorally disturbed child with parents as therapists. *Journal of Behavior Therapy and Experimental Psychiatry, 9,* 65-70.

Johnson, R. J. (1990). Introduction to the special issue on the creative arts therapies with adolescents. *The Arts in Psychotherapy, 17,* 97-99.

Johnson, T. C. (1988). Child perpetrators—Children who molest other children: Preliminary findings. *Child Abuse & Neglect, 12,* 219-229.

Johnson, T. C. (1989). Female child perpetrators: Children who molest other children. *Child Abuse & Neglect, 13,* 571-585.

Johnson, T. C., & Aoki, W. T. (1993). Sexual behaviors in latency age children in residential treatment. *Residential Treatment for Children & Youth, 11,* 1-22.

Jones, R. N., & Downing, R. H. (1991). Assessment of the use of timeout in an inpatient child psychiatry treatment unit. *Behavioral Residential Treatment, 6,* 219-230.

Kagan, R. M. (1993). Professional development for a therapeutic environment. In C. E. Schaefer & A. J. Swanson (Eds.), *Children in residential care: Critical issues in treatment* (pp. 160-174). Northvale, NJ: Jason Aronson.

Kaplan, H. I., & Sadock, B. J. (1985). *Modern synopsis of comprehensive textbook of psychiatry/IV.* Baltimore: Williams & Wilkins.

Katz, M. (1993). Crisis intervention in residential care. In C. E. Schaefer & A. J. Swanson (Eds.), *Children in residential care: Critical issues in treatment* (pp. 30-49). Northvale, NJ: Jason Aronson.

Kazdin, A. E. (1977). *The token economy.* New York: Plenum.

Kazdin, A. E., Bass, D., Ayers, W. A., & Rodgers, A. (1990). Empirical and clinical focus of child and adolescent psychotherapy research. *Journal of Consulting and Clinical Psychology, 58,* 729-740.

Keith-Lucas, A. (1987). What else can residential care do? And do well? *Residential Treatment for Children & Youth, 4,* 25-37.

Kelly, F. (1974, Oct.). Outward bound and delinquency: A ten-year experience. Paper presented at the Conference on Experimental Education. Estes Park, CO.

Kelly, F., & Baer, D. (1968). *Outward bound schools as an alternative to institutionalization for adolescent delinquent boys.* Boston: Fardel.

Kendall, P. C., & Finch, A. J. (1978). A cognitive-behavioral treatment for impulsivity: A group comparison study. *Journal of Consulting and Clinical Psychology, 46,* 110-118.

Kerlinsky, D. (1991). Integrating interdisciplinary team-centered treatment. In R. L. Hendren & I. N. Berlin (Eds.), *Psychiatric inpatient care of children and adolescents: A multicultural approach* (pp. 93-111). New York: Wiley.

Kifer, R. E., Lewis, M. A., Green, D. R., & Phillips, E. C. (1974). Training predelinquent youths and their parents to negotiate conflict situations. *Journal of Applied Behavior Analysis, 7,* 357-364.

Kinney, J. M., Madsen, B., Fleming, T., & Haapala, D. A. (1977). Homebuilders: Keeping families together. *Journal of Consulting and Clinical Psychology, 45,* 667-673.

Kirigin, K. A., Braukmann, C. J., Atwater, J. D., & Wolf, M. M. (1982). An evaluation of teaching-family (Achievement Place) group houses for juvenile offenders. *Journal of Applied Behavior Analysis, 15,* 1-16.

Kirk, S. A. (1972). *Educating exceptional children* (2nd ed.). Boston: Houghton Mifflin.

Koocher, G. P. (1976). A bill of rights for children in psychotherapy. In G. P. Koocher (Ed.), *Children's rights and the mental health professions* (pp. 23-32). New York: Wiley.

Koocher, G. P., & Keith-Spiegel, P. C. (1990). *Children, ethics, and the law: Professional issues and cases.* Lincoln: University of Nebraska Press.

Kramer, D. T. (1994). *Legal rights of children: Volumes 1, 2, 3* (2nd ed.). New York: McGraw-Hill.

Krona, D. A. (1980). Parents as treatment partners in residential care. *Child Welfare, 59,* 91-96.

Krumboltz, J. D., & Krumboltz, H. B. (1972). *Changing children's behavior.* Englewood Cliffs, NJ: Prentice Hall.

Kuster, T., Rowland, G., Schaeffner, T., & Kupfersmid, J. (1988). Strategies for the prevention of physical assault among emotionally disturbed youths (P.A.A.R.R.). *Child & Youth Services, 10*, 85-99.

Lambert, P. (1977). *The ABCs of child care work in residential care: The Linden Hill manual.* New York: Child Welfare League.

Lane, D. (1993). Under what circumstances should children be referred to residential settings? *Child & Youth Care Forum, 22*, 103-109.

Lazarus, A. (1960). The elimination of children's phobias by deconditioning. In H. J. Eysenck (Ed.), *Behavior therapy and the neuroses* (pp. 114-122). New York: Pergamon.

LeCroy, C. W. (1988). Anger management or anger expression: Which is most effective? *Residential Treatment for Children & Youth, 5*, 29-39.

Levitt, E. E. (1971). Research on psychotherapy with children. In A. E. Bergin & S. Garfield (Eds.), *Handbook of psychotherapy and behavior change* (pp. 474-494). New York: Wiley.

Lewis, M., Lewis, D. O., Shanock, S. S., Klatskin, E., & Osborne, J. R. (1980). The undoing of residential treatment: A follow-up study of 51 adolescents. *Journal of the American Academy of Child Psychiatry, 19*, 160-171.

Lewis, M., & Summerville, J. W. (1991). Residential treatment. In M. Lewis (Ed.), *Child and adolescent psychiatry: A comprehensive textbook* (pp. 895-902). Baltimore: Williams & Wilkins.

Lewis, W. W. (1988). The role of ecological variables in residential treatment. *Behavior Disorders, 13*, 98-107.

Loughmiller, C. (1965). *Wilderness road.* Austin: University of Texas Press.

Lovaas, O. I. (1978). Parents as therapists. In M. Rutter & E. Scopler (Eds.), *Autism: A reappraisal of concepts and treatment* (pp. 369-378). New York: Plenum.

Lovaas, O. I. (1987). Behavioral treatment and normal educational and intellectual functioning in young autistic children. *Journal of Consulting and Clinical Psychology, 55*, 3-9.

Lovaas, O. I., Freitag, L., Nelson, K., & Whalen, C. (1967). The establishment of imitation and its use for the development of complex behavior in schizophrenic children. *Behavior Research and Therapy, 5*, 171-181.

Lyman, R. D. (1984). The effects of private and public goal setting on classroom on-task behavior of emotionally disturbed children. *Behavior Therapy, 15*, 395-402.

Lyman, R. D., Prentice-Dunn, S., & Wilson, D. R. (1995). Behavioral day treatment as an alternative to residential or inpatient treatment. *Continuum, 2*, 71-83.

Lyman, R. D., Prentice-Dunn, S., Wilson, D. R., & Taylor, G. E., Jr. (1989). Issues in residential and inpatient treatment. In R. D. Lyman, S. Prentice-Dunn, & S. Gabel (Eds.), *Residential and inpatient treatment of children and adolescents* (pp. 3-22). New York: Plenum.

Lyth, I. M. (1985). The development of the self in children in institutions. *Journal of Child Psychotherapy, 11*, 49-64.

Maas, K., & Ney, D. (1992). Suicide in residential care: Implications for child care staff. *Journal of Child and Youth Care, 7*, 45-57.

Magnus, R. A. (1974, January-February). Teaching parents to parent: Parent involvement in residential treatment programs. *Children Today*, pp. 25-27.

Maier, H. W. (1975). Learning to live and living to learn in residential treatment. *Child Welfare, 54*, 406-420.

Maluccio, A. N. (1993). Promoting permanency planning. In C. E. Schaefer & A. J. Swanson (Eds.), *Children in residential care: Critical issues in treatment* (pp. 175-190). Northvale, NJ: Jason Aronson.

Margolis, R. B., Sorensen, J. L., & Galano, J. (1977). Consumer satisfaction in mental health delivery services. *Professional Psychology, 8,* 11-16.

Masters, K. J., & Devany, J. (1992). Are physical restraints necessary? *Journal of the American Academy of Child and Adolescent Psychiatry, 31,* 372.

Mazzarins, H., Payne, M., & Kupfersmid, J. (1988). Utilizing mechanical restraints. *Child & Youth Services, 10,* 153-163.

McFadden, E. J. (1992). The inner world of children and youth in care. *Community Alternatives, 4,* 1-17.

McGrath, T. (1991). Overcoming institutionalized child abuse: Creating a positive therapeutic climate. *Journal of Child and Youth Care, 6,* 61-68.

McNeil, E. (1962). Forty years of childhood: The University of Michigan Fresh Air Camp, 1921-1961. *Michigan Quarterly Review, 1,* 112-118.

Mercer, M. (1982). Closing the barn door: The prevention of institutional abuse through standards. *Child & Youth Services, 4,* 127-132.

Miller, D. E. (1986). The management of misbehavior by seclusion. *Residential Treatment for Children & Youth, 4,* 63-72.

Miller, D., & Burt, R. A. (1982). Children's rights on entering therapeutic institutions. *Children & Youth Services, 4,* 89-98.

Miller, D., Walker, M., & Friedman, D. (1989). Use of a holding technique to control the violent behavior of seriously disturbed adolescents. *Hospital and Community Psychiatry, 40,* 520-524.

Millstein, K. H., & Cotton, N. S. (1990). Predictors of the use of seclusion on an inpatient child psychiatric unit. *Journal of the American Academy of Child and Adolescent Psychiatry, 29,* 256-264.

Monkman, M. (1972). *A milieu therapy program for behaviorally disturbed children.* Springfield, IL: Charles C Thomas.

Mordock, J. B. (1993). Evaluating treatment effectiveness. In C. E. Schaefer & A. J. Swanson (Eds.), *Children in residential care: Critical issues in treatment* (pp. 219-250). Northvale, NJ: Jason Aronson.

Moss, G. R. (1994). A biobehavioral perspective on the hospital treatment of adolescents. In P. W. Corrigan & R. P. Liberman (Eds.), *Behavior therapy in psychiatric hospitals* (pp. 109-127). New York: Springer.

Murray, L., & Sefchik, G. (1992). Regulating behavior management practices in residential treatment facilities. *Children and Youth Services Review, 14,* 519-539.

Natta, M. B., Holmbeck, G. N., Kupst, M. J., Pines, R. J., & Schulman, J. L. (1990). Sequences of staff-child interactions on a psychiatric inpatient unit. *Journal of Abnormal Child Psychology, 18,* 1-14.

Nevin, D. A. (1993). Staff training needs around sex abuse in residential treatment. In W. de C. Braga & R. Schimmer (Eds.), *Sexual abuse and residential treatment* (pp. 63-80). New York: Haworth.

Ney, P. G., & Mulvihill, D. L. (1985). *Child psychiatric treatment: A practical guide.* Dover, NJ: Croom Helm.

Palmer, T. (1974). The Youth Authority's Community Treatment Project. *Federal Probation, 38,* 3-14.

Pardeck, J. T. (1992). Using bibliotherapy in treatment with children in residential care. *Residential Treatment for Children & Youth, 9,* 73-90.

Patterson, G. (1976). The aggressive child: Victim and architect of a coercive system. In E. Mash, L. Hamerlynck, & L. Handy (Eds.), *Behavior modification and families: Theory and research* (pp. 131-158). New York: Brunner/Mazel.

Pecora, P. J., Fraser, M. W., & Haapala, D. A. (1992). Intensive home-base family preservation services: An update from the FIT Project. *Child Welfare, 71,* 177-188.

Pfeffer, C. R. (1989). Assessment of suicidal children and adolescents. *Psychiatric Clinics of North America, 12,* 861-872.

Pfeffer, C. R., Plutchik, R., & Mizruchi, S. (1986). A comparison of psychopathology in child psychiatric inpatients, outpatients, and nonpatients: Implications for treatment planning. *Journal of Nervous and Mental Disease, 174,* 529-535.

Pfeiffer, S. I. (1989). Follow-up of children and adolescents treated in psychiatric facilities: A methodology review. *Psychiatric Hospital, 20,* 15-20.

Pfeiffer, S. I., & Strzelecki, S. C. (1990). Inpatient psychiatric treatment of children and adolescents: A review of outcome studies. *Journal of the American Academy of Child and Adolescent Psychiatry, 29,* 847-853.

Phillips, E. L., Phillips, E. A., Fixsen, D. L., & Wolf, M. M. (1971). Achievement Place: Modification of the behaviors of predelinquent boys within a token economy. *Journal of Applied Behavior Analysis, 4,* 45-59.

Phillips, E. L., Phillips, E. A., Wolf, M. M., & Fixsen, D. L. (1973). Achievement Place: Development of the elected manager system. *Journal of Applied Behavior Analysis, 6,* 541-563.

Pierce, L. H. (1985). Selecting children for residential treatment. *Children and Youth Services, 7,* 299-308.

Ploufe, M. M. (1981). A longitudinal analysis of the personality and behavioral effects of participation in the Connecticut Wilderness School: A program for delinquent and pre-delinquent youth. (Doctoral dissertation, University of Connecticut, 1981). *Dissertation Abstracts International, 41*(12-B), 4683.

Polsky, H. W. (1962). *Cottage six: The social system of delinquent boys in residential treatment.* New York: Russell Sage Foundation.

Polsky, H. W., & Claster, D. S. (1968). *The dynamics of residential treatment: A social system analysis.* Chapel Hill: University of North Carolina Press.

Prentice-Dunn, S., Wilson, D. R., & Lyman, R. D. (1981). Client factors related to outcome in a residential and day treatment program for children. *Journal of Clinical Child Psychology, 10,* 188-191.

Pro-Ed. (1991). *Tests: A comprehensive reference for assessment in psychology, education, and business* (3rd ed.). Austin, TX: Author.

Quay, H. (1986). Residential treatment. In H. Quay & J. S. Wherry (Eds.), *Psychopathological disorders of childhood* (3rd ed., pp. 558-580). New York: Wiley.

Raush, H. L., Dittman, A. T., & Taylor, J. J. (1959). The interpersonal behavior of children in residential treatment. *Journal of Abnormal and Social Psychology, 58,* 9-26.

Ravenscroft, K. (1991). Family therapy. In M. Lewis (Ed.), *Child and adolescent psychiatry: A comprehensive textbook* (pp. 850-898). Baltimore: Williams & Wilkins.

Redl, F. (1966). *When we deal with children.* New York: Free Press.

Redl, F., & Wineman, D. (1957). *The aggressive child.* New York: Free Press.

Richards, A. (1981). *Kurt Hahn: The midwife of educational ideas.* Unpublished doctoral dissertation, University of Colorado, Boulder.

Rickard, H. C., & Dinoff, M. (Eds.). (1974). *Behavior modification in children: Case studies and illustrations from a summer camp.* University: University of Alabama Press.

Rindfleisch, N. (1993). Combating institutional abuse. In C. E. Schaefer & A. J. Swanson (Eds.), *Children in residential care: Critical issues in treatment* (pp. 263-283). Northvale, NJ: Jason Aronson.

Rindfleisch, N., & Baros-Van Hull, J. (1982). Direct care workers' attitudes toward use of physical force with children. *Child & Youth Services, 4,* 115-125.

Robin, M. (1982). The abuse of status offenders in private hospitals. *Child & Youth Services, 4,* 79-87.

Rogers-Warren, A., & Baer, D. M. (1976). Correspondence between saying and doing: Teaching children to share and praise. *Journal of Applied Behavior Analysis, 9,* 335-354.

Rosenthal, F., & Pinsky, G. (1936). Follow-up method in child guidance work. *American Journal of Orthopsychiatry, 6,* 609-615.

Ross, A. L., & Hoeltke, G. (1985). A tool for selecting residential child care workers: An initial report. *Child Welfare, 64,* 46-54.

Ross, A. O. (1964). Learning theory and therapy with children. *Psychotherapy: Theory, Research and Practice, 1,* 102-108.

Saigh, P. A. (1989). A comparative analysis of the affective and behavioral symptomology of traumatized and nontraumatized children. *Journal of School Psychology, 27,* 247-255.

Satir, V. (1967). *Conjoint family therapy: A guide to theory and technique* (rev. ed.). Palo Alto, CA: Science and Behavior Books.

Schaefer, C. E., & Swanson, A. J. (Eds.). (1993). *Children in residential care: Critical issues in treatment.* Northvale, NJ: Jason Aronson.

Schain, R. J., Gardella, D., & Pon, J. (1982). Five year outcome of children admitted to a state hospital. *Hospital and Community Psychiatry, 33,* 847-848.

Scheirer, M. A., & Rezmovic, E. L. (1983). Measuring the degree of program implementation. *Evaluation Review, 7,* 599-633.

Schimmer, R. (1993). Dangerous development: Considerations concerning the governance of sexual behavior in residential treatment centers. In W. de C. Braga & R. Schimmer (Eds.), *Sexual abuse and residential treatment* (pp. 23-34). New York: Haworth.

Schneider, B. H. (1991). A comparison of skill-building and desensitization strategies for intervention with aggressive children. *Aggressive Behavior, 17,* 301-311.

Schneider, M., & Robin, A. (1976). The turtle technique: A method for the self-control of impulsive behavior. In J. D. Krumboltz & C. G. Thoresen (Eds), *Counseling methods* (pp. 157-162). New York: Holt, Rinehart & Winston.

Schultz, J. M., & Dark, S. L. (1982). *Manual of psychiatric nursing care plans.* Boston: Little, Brown.

Schultz, M. J. (1991). Program development and training in residential treatment: Integrating milieu and systemic models. *Journal of Strategic and Systemic Therapies, 10,* 6-20.

Shealy, C. N. (1995). From Boys Town to Oliver Twist: Separating fact from fiction in welfare reform and out-of-home placement of children and youth. *American Psychologist, 50,* 565-580.

Silver, S. E., Duchnowski, A. J., Kutash, K., Friedman, R. M., Eisen, M., Prange, M. E., Brandenburg, N. A., & Greenbaum, P. E. (1992). A comparison of children with serious emotional disturbance served in residential and school settings. *Journal of Child and Family Studies, 1,* 43-59.

Slaby, A. E., & McGuire, P. L. (1989). Residential management of suicidal adolescents. *Residential Treatment for Children and Youth, 7,* 23-43.

Small, M. A., & Otto, R. K. (1991). Utilizing the "professional judgment standard" in child advocacy. *Journal of Clinical Child Psychology, 20,* 71-77.

Small, R. W., & Schinke, S. P. (1983). Teaching competence in residential group care: Cognitive problem solving and interpersonal skills training with emotionally disturbed preadolescents. *Journal of Social Service Research, 7,* 1-16.

Small, R., Kennedy, K., & Bender, B. (1991). Critical issues for practice in residential treatment: The view from within. *American Journal of Orthopsychiatry, 61,* 327-338.

Smith, P. A. (1991). Time-out and seclusion: Understanding the civil rights and treatment issues. *Residential Treatment for Children & Youth, 9,* p. 60.

Spence, S. H., & Marzillier, J. S. (1981). Social skills training with adolescent male offenders: Short-term, long-term, and generalized effects. *Behavior Research and Therapy, 19,* 349-368.

Spitz, R. A. (1945). Hospitalism: An inquiry into the genesis of psychiatric conditions in early childhood. *Psycho-analytic Study of the Child, 1,* 53-74.

Stearns, F. A. (1991). Inpatient group treatment of children and adolescents. In R. L. Hendren & I. N. Berlin (Eds.), *Psychiatric inpatient care of children and adolescents: A multicultural approach* (pp. 112-126). New York: Wiley.

Steinberg, D., Galhenage, D. P. C., & Robinson, S. C. (1981). Two years' referrals to a regional adolescent unit: Some implications for psychiatric services. *Social Science of Medicine, 15E,* 113-122.

Stuart, R. B. (1971). Behavioral contracting within the families of delinquents. *Journal of Behavior Therapy and Experimental Psychiatry, 2,* 1-11.

Swanson, A. J., & Richard, B. A. (1993). Discipline and child behavior management in group care. In C. E. Schaefer & A. J. Swanson (Eds.), *Children in residential care: Critical issues in treatment* (pp. 77-88). Northvale, NJ: Jason Aronson.

Swanson, A. J., & Schaefer, C. E. (1993). Helping children deal with separation and loss in residential placement. In C. E. Schaefer & A. J. Swanson (Eds.), *Children in residential care: Critical issues in treatment* (pp. 19-29). Northvale, NJ: Jason Aronson.

Taylor, D. A., & Alpert, S. W. (1973). *Continuity and support following residential treatment.* New York: Child Welfare League.

Thies, A. P. (1976). The facts of life: Child advocacy and children's rights in residential treatment. In G. P. Koocher (Ed.), *Children's rights and the mental health professions* (pp. 85-96). New York: Wiley.

Thomas, G. (1982). The responsibility of residential placements for children's rights to development. *Child & Youth Services, 4,* 23-45.

Thomas, G. (1989). Keeping children's needs paramount: A new era of accountability and opportunity for group residential services. *Child & Youth Care Quarterly, 18,* 81-92.

Titus, R. (1989). Therapeutic crisis intervention training at Kinark Child and Family Services. *Journal of Child and Youth Care, 4,* 61-71.

Trieschman, A. E., Whittaker, J. K., & Brendtro, L. K. (1969). *The other 23 hours.* Chicago: Aldine.

Tsemberis, S., & Sullivan, C. (1988). Seclusion in context: Introducing a seclusion room into a children's unit of a municipal hospital. *American Journal of Orthopsychiatry, 58,* 462-465.

Tuma, J. M. (1989). Mental health services for children. *American Psychologist, 44,* 188-199.

VanDenBerg, J. E. (1993). Integration of individualized mental health services into the system of care for children and adolescents. *Administration and Policy in Mental Health, 20,* 247-257.

Vargas, L. A., & Berlin, I. N. (1991). Culturally responsive inpatient care of children and adolescents. In R. L. Hendren & I. N. Berlin (Eds.), *Psychiatric inpatient care of children and adolescents: A multicultural approach* (pp. 14-33). New York: Wiley.

Velasquez, J. S., & Lyle, C. G. (1985). Day versus residential treatment for juvenile offenders: The impact of program evaluation. *Child Welfare, 64,* 145-156.

Vorrath, H. H., & Brendtro, L. K. (1974). *Positive peer culture.* Chicago: Aldine.

Warren, M. Q. (1969). The case for differential treatment of delinquents. *Annals of the American Academy of Political and Social Science, 38,* 47-59.

Weinrott, M. R., Jones, R. R., & Howard, J. R. (1982). Cost-effectiveness of teaching family programs for delinquents: Results of a national evaluation. *Evaluation Review, 6,* 173-201.

Weinstein, L. (1969). Project Re-Ed schools for emotionally disturbed children: Effectiveness as viewed by referring agencies, parents, and teachers. *Exceptional Children, 35,* 703-711.

Weinstein, L. (1974). *Evaluation of a program for re-educating disturbed children: A follow-up comparison with untreated children* (Final Report to the Bureau for the Education of the Handicapped, Project Nos. 6-2974, 552023). Washington, DC: U.S. Department of Health, Education & Welfare.

Weisz, J. R., Walter, B. R., Weiss, B., Fernandez, G. A., & Mikow, V. A. (1990). Arrests among emotionally disturbed violent and assaultive individuals following minimal versus lengthy intervention through North Carolina's Willie M. Program. *Journal of Consulting and Clinical Psychology, 58,* 720-728.

Weisz, J. R., & Weiss, B. (1993). *Effects of psychotherapy with children and adolescents.* Newbury Park, CA: Sage.

Weisz, J. R., Weiss, B., Alicke, M. D., & Klotz, M. L. (1987). Effectiveness of psychotherapy with children and adolescents: A meta-analysis for clinicians. *Journal of Consulting and Clinical Psychology, 55,* 542-549.

Weisz, J. R., Weiss, B., Morton, T., Granger, D., & Han, S. (1992). *Meta-analysis of psychotherapy outcome research with children and adolescents.* Unpublished manuscript, University of California, Los Angeles.

Weithorn, L. A. (1988). Mental hospitalization of troublesome youth: An analysis of skyrocketing admission rates. *Harvard Law Review, 40,* 773-838.

Wells, K. (1991). Placement of emotionally disturbed children in residential treatment: A review of placement criteria. *American Journal of Orthopsychiatry, 61,* 339-347.

Wells, K., & Whittington, D. (1993). Characteristics of youths referred to residential treatment: Implications for program design. *Children and Youth Services Review, 15,* 195-217.

Wherry, J. N. (1986). The therapeutic use of seclusion with children and adolescents. *Residential Treatment for Children & Youth, 4,* 51-61.

Whitehead, J. T., & Lab, S. P. (1989). A meta-analysis of juvenile correctional treatment. *Journal of Research in Crime and Delinquency, 26,* 276-295.

Whittaker, J. K. (1979). *Caring for troubled children.* San Francisco: Jossey-Bass.

Whittaker, J. K., & Pecora, P. (1984). A research agenda for residential care. In T. Philpot (Ed.), *Group care practice: The challenge of the next decade* (pp. 71-86). Surrey, UK: Business Press International.

Whittaker, J. K., Fine, D., & Grasso, A. (1989). Characteristics of adolescents and their families in residential treatment intake: An exploratory study. In E. Balcerzak (Ed.), *Group care of children: Transition toward the year 2000* (pp. 67-87). Washington, DC: Child Welfare League.

Wiener, J. M. (1985). *Diagnosis and psychopharmacology of childhood and adolescent disorders.* New York: Wiley.

Wilman, H. C., & Chunn, F. Y. (1973). Homeward bound: An alternative to the institutionalization of adjudicated juvenile offenders. *Federal Probation, 37,* 52-57.

Wilson, D. R., & Lyman, R. D. (1982). Time-out in the treatment of childhood behavior problems: Implementation and research. *Child and Family Behavior Therapy, 4,* 5-20.

Wilson, D. R., & Lyman, R. D. (1983). Residential treatment of emotionally disturbed children. In C. E. Walker & M. E. Roberts (Eds.), *Handbook of clinical child psychology* (pp. 1064-1088). New York: Wiley.

Winsberg, B. G., Bialer, I., Kupietz, S., Botti, E., & Balka, E. B. (1980). Home vs. hospital care of children with behavior disorders: A controlled investigation. *Archives of General Psychiatry, 37,* 412-418.

Wodarski, J. S., Feldman, R. A., & Pedi, S. J. (1974). Objective measurement of the independent variable: A neglected methodological aspect in community-based behavioral research. *Journal of Abnormal Child Psychology, 2,* 239-244.

Wolf, F. M. (1986). *Meta-analysis: Quantitative methods for research synthesis.* Beverly Hills, CA: Sage.

Wolpe, J. (1958). *Psychotherapy by reciprocal inhibition.* Stanford, CA: Stanford University Press.

Woolston, J. L. (1991). Psychiatric inpatient services for children. In M. Lewis (Ed.), *Child and adolescent psychiatry: A comprehensive textbook* (pp. 890-894). Baltimore: Williams & Wilkins.

Wurtele, S. K., Wilson, D. R., & Prentice-Dunn, S. (1983). Characteristics of children in residential treatment programs: Findings and implications. *Journal of Clinical Child Psychology, 12,* 137-144.

Young, R. A. (1939). A summer camp as an integral part of a psychiatric clinic. *Mental Hygiene, 23,* 241-256.

Yuan, Y. T., McDonald, W. R., Wheeler, C. E., Struckman-Johnson, D., & Rivest, M. (1990). Evaluation of AB1562 in-home care projects: Final report. (vols. 1 and 2). Sacramento, CA: Walter R. McDonald and Associates.

Zahn, B. S. (1991). The survivors project: A new multimodal therapy program for adolescents who have survived child sexual abuse. In *Contributions to residential treatment, 1991* (pp. 107-123). Washington, DC: American Association of Children's Residential Centers.

Zimmerman, D. P. (1994). A pilot demographic study of population changes in a residential treatment center. *Residential Treatment for Children & Youth, 11,* 17-32.

NAME INDEX

A.D.D. Warehouse, 106
Achievement Place, 13, 20, 81
Adams, R., 86
Adolescence, 104
Adoption and Fostering, 104
Adult Children Anonymous (ACA), 113
Aggression Replacement Training
  (ART), 38
Aichorn, A., 11
Alabama, 29
Alanon Family Group (AFG), 113
Alanon, 113
Alateen, 113
Alcoholics Anonymous World Services
  (AA), 113
Aldgate, J., 67
Allerhand, M. E., 76
American Association of Children's
  Residential Treatment Centers
  (AACRC), 101
American Association of Psychiatric
  Services for Children (AAPSC),
  102
American Bar Association Center on
  Children and the Law (ABACCL),
  119
American Foster Care Resources
  (AFCR), 116
American Guidance Service, 110
American Journal of Orthopsychiatry,
  104
American Journal of Psychiatry, 104
American Professional Society on the
  Abuse of Children, 119
American Psychiatric Association, 26, 63

American Psychological Association
  (APA), 102, 103, 104
  Child maltreatment section of, 102
  Child, Youth, and Family Services
    division of, 102
  Clinical child psychology subdivision
    of, 102
  Clinical psychology division of, 102
  Family Psychology division of, 102
Angold, A., 58, 59, 70
Aoki, W. T., 66, 67
*APA Ethical Principles of Psychologists
  and Code of Conduct,* 104
Axline, V. M., 5
Azrin, N. H., 5, 21

Bacon, S. B., 85
Barber, C. C., 66
Barker, P., 1, 2, 3, 4, 30, 32, 40, 52
Barton, C., 83
Basta, J. M., 85
Bath, H. I., 97
Batterers Anonymous, 115
Beker, J., 49, 51, 52
Bellefaire, 76
Bereika, G. M., 26, 44
Berlin, I. N., 32, 35
Beskind, H., 75
Bettelheim, B., 2, 11, 17, 21
Bibliotherapy for Children, 107
Blair, D. T., 58, 62, 68, 69
Blase, K. A., 13
Bleiberg, E., 45, 48, 49
Blotcky, J. M., 84, 85

SUBJECT INDEX

Centers. *See* Programs
Characteristics of children served, 18
Characteristics of clients, 32, 48, 50
  See also Child abuse; Demographics;
    Diagnoses
Chemical dependency, 113-114
  See also Substance abuse
Child abuse, 29, 59, 92, 93, 96, 97, 98,
    115
  background of, 27, 28, 29, 30, 43,
    48-49, 58
  prevention of, 42, 46, 48-49, 66-68
  reporting, 47
  therapy for, 37, 39
Child and family characteristics, 74-75,
    88
Child guidance model, 12
Child neglect, 92, 97, 98
Child psychiatric inpatient units, 13
  See also Inpatient facilities
Child welfare. *See* System of care
Children:
  community-based treatment for, 95-96
  day treatment for, 92, 94
  investment in treatment, 91
  treatment of, 77-79, 83-85, 87
  See also Developmental issues
Chores, 52
Clientele. *See* Characteristics of clients;
    Demographics; Diagnoses
Clinical psychology, 33
Clinical social work. *See* Social work
Co-dependency, 118
Cognitive-behavioral interventions, 86
  See also Therapy
Cohesion, 52, 55, 69
  See also Staffing
Communication, 52, 54-55, 56-57, 60,
    62, 65-66, 68, 69, 70
  See also Staffing
Community involvement, 22-23, 25, 41,
    50, 69, 96
Community-based treatment, 3, 94-99
  cost savings, 96, 99
Complete vs. incomplete treatment, 82
Conduct disorders. *See* Diagnoses
Confidentiality, 47-48, 70
Consistency, 52

  See also Structure
Consultation, 31, 32, 34-35, 40-41, 43
Consumer satisfaction, 72
Contingency management, 81, 86, 90
  applied to academic performance, 20
Continuum of care, 5-9, 24, 25, 98, 99
Control groups, 74, 80
Cooperation, 52, 55
  See also Staffing
Coping, 41, 43, 58
Cost:
  effectiveness, 23, 25
  of day treatment vs. inpatient
    treatment, 93
  of psychiatric inpatient care, 14
  See also Funding
Counseling, 33
  See also Therapy
Crisis intervention, 37, 40, 43, 52, 57-70,
    96, 99
Criterion drift, 72
Custody, 115-116

Day treatment, 6, 89-94, 99
  advantages over outpatient treatment,
    90
  advantages over residential treatment,
    90
  behavioral, 92
  efficacy, 91
  outcome, 91-94
  safety, 91, 94
  staff, 91
  stigmatization in, 91
Debriefing, 56
De-escalation, 54, 62
  See also Behavior management;
    Communication
Delinquency
  community-based treatment for, 94,
    95, 96, 97
  predicting outcome from, 97
  treatment of, 80, 81, 82, 83, 85, 86,
    88, 92, 94
  See also Parole, System of care,
    Juvenile correctional institutions
Demographics, 26-30, 43

ABOUT THE AUTHORS

Robert D. Lyman is Professor of Psychology and Executive Director of Brewer-Porch Children's Center at the University of Alabama, Tuscaloosa, Alabama. Brewer-Porch Children's Center is a teaching, service, and research program in the area of child and adolescent emotional and behavioral disorders operated by the University of Alabama. He received his bachelor's degree in psychology from Brown University and his master's and PhD degrees in clinical psychology from the University of Alabama. Prior to assuming his present position, he was Chief Child Psychologist, Department of Psychiatry, University of Alabama Medical Center, Birmingham, Alabama. His primary research and clinical interests are in the areas of behavior therapy, residential treatment, and clinical neuropsychology.

Nancy R. Campbell is Coordinator of Psychology Services at Brewer-Porch Children's Center and has an adjunct appointment as Associate Professor in the Department of Psychology at the University of Alabama. Prior to assuming this position, she was Professor of Psychology at Birmingham-Southern College where, in 1992, she received their Excellence in Teaching Award. A Phi Beta Kappa graduate of Florida State University and winner of the Martin S. Wallach Award for the Outstanding Clinical Psychology Intern at the University of North Carolina at Chapel Hill, she completed her PhD in clinical psychology at the University of Alabama, Tuscaloosa. Her clinical interests include assessment of childhood psychopathology and inpatient treatment of severely disturbed children.

149